I WAS
LOOKING
FOR A
STREET

CHARLES WILLEFORD

I WAS LOOKING FOR A STREET

THE COUNTRYMAN PRESS
WOODSTOCK, VERMONT

First Edition

Copyright © 1988 by Charles Willeford

Library of Congress Cataloging in Publication Data
Willeford, Charles Ray, 1919–1988
   I was looking for a street / Charles Willeford. — 1st ed.
     p.   cm.
   ISBN 0-88150-112-3 : $14.95
   1. Willeford, Charles Ray, 1919–1988—Biography—Youth.
2. Authors, American—20th century—Biography. 3.
Tramps—United States—Biography. 4. Los Angeles
(Calif.)—Social life and customs.   I. Title.
PS3545.I464Z465   1988
813'.54—dc19
[B]   88-413
                                           CIP

Book design by Ann Aspell
Frontispiece by Dee Clark
Typesetting by N.K. Graphics
Printed in the United States of America
by Arcata Graphics

The Countryman Press

Woodstock, Vermont
05091

For euphonious reasons, most of the names, but
not all of them, have been changed in this book.

—C.W.

For Robert D. Loomis

After the overture,
The opera seemed brief.

—Donald Justice

PERFORCE

Am I the guilty stone in the avalanche?
Did I take the other road?
The grinning violence of a small death
I revitalize in half-blind driving,
Marking ghostly landmarks, haze-hidden points,
Unclosed parentheses, Indelible sitzmarks—
                    Unlimited tolls.

But this one, I know, is a toll-free call,
A long distance surprise like a pressed flower
In a calf-bound dictionary
Between "Corinth" and "Cornucopia."

So I will inch painfully down
The splintered pole of memory
Where we can meet each other again,
When I was more unaware than wary.

PART ONE

OVERTURE

1

I don't think we were rich, or anything close to that, but we were well-to-do. We lived in a big two-story house in Topanga Canyon, which was still open country then, and everyone in the family was working except me. My grandmother, Mattie Sawyers, worked six days a week at the May Company in downtown Los Angeles, selling millinery in the French Room. My uncle Roy, Mattie's son, worked for Southwestern Bell, and he owned a new Model A Ford. My mother, Aileen, who had been widowed since my second birthday, had remarried, and her new husband, Joe Cassidy, owned a garage on Western Avenue. In addition to renting parking spaces, Joe did mechanical work at the garage, and he also held several points in a shock absorber he had helped invent. My mother, who had graduated from Boscobel College in Tennesse with a degree in music, taught piano, voice, and expression in our home in Topanga Canyon. So altogether, there was a good deal of money coming into that house every month.

We had a full-time Negro cook, and we ate big dinners at night—huge roasts, turkeys, chicken and dumplings, and I don't remember what all. Except for Joe Cassidy, who had moved to Los Angeles from New York City, Mattie, Mama, and Roy were from Greenville, Mississippi, so southern cooking predominated. Because I was the only child, and a boy at that, I was indulged. I liked Jell-O, for example, and regardless of the desserts the others had, I was always served Jell-O, usually the red kind with chopped bananas in it. I was also a finicky eater for a boy of seven, so each evening meal was preceded by a tablespoon of "Beef Wine & Iron" tonic, which was supposed to stimulate my appetite. I hated the taste of this tonic, but I rarely got out of taking it.

Joe Cassidy, who had married my mother—not me—didn't like me very much, but everyone else, including our cook, loved me. I had a bicycle, an Erector set, an electric train, toys of all kinds, and it was always summertime in Topanga, as I recall, because I didn't go to school. After breakfast, I rode my bike down the highway for about a mile and spent the morning in a public pool. I rode back for lunch, and afterward, when my mother's students came to the house for lessons, I played outside with the kids who were waiting for their turns at the piano. I giggled a lot during the voice and expression lessons, especially when some little girl would recite the "poor little worm" piece.

"Poor little worm," the girl would address the imaginary worm in her palm, "d'you wanna see God?" Then she would crush the worm in her hand, grinning with malice.

Every six weeks or so, Mama gave recitals in a rented church auditorium, with all of the parents of her students and their friends in the audience. I would sit in the back with Mattie, but Joe Cassidy and Uncle Roy didn't come to these student recitals.

When I was six, my mother had tried to give me piano lessons but I refused to take them. After two or three attempts, she gave up. She taught me how to sing two songs, however, "Freckles," and "Mighty Like A Rose," which I learned by heart. She accompanied me on the piano, and after I got these two songs perfected, including the hand and arm gestures, she curled my straight blond hair into tight little ringlets. I couldn't sit still, and the smell of the cooking hair made me cry. My hair was curled anyway, and I got a couple of painful scalp burns from the hot iron. A few bad days came then, but there weren't many of them. My mother didn't drive, so we had to take buses and streetcars, making several transfers, and then we waited—it seemed like hours—in movie studio waiting rooms. My turn would come, and I would sing my two songs to some indifferent man behind a desk while my mother accompanied me on the office upright. I wore a black velvet Lord Fauntleroy suit with short pants, a white waist (they weren't called shirts), a black string tie, white socks, and black patent-leather shoes. I was a pretty but sullen-mouthed kid, and nothing ever came from these auditions. I hated the curls, the long tiring bus and streetcar rides, the stuffy waiting rooms filled with shushed kids, and singing to strange men who almost always smoked smelly cigars while I sang my two songs. My mother was never discouraged, though. As she told Mattie, the fact that I was allowed to sing both songs, instead of being dismissed after the first, was a favorable sign of my talent.

But there were only four or five of these trips. My mother had tuberculosis and she was dying. She wasn't strong enough physically to keep taking me around to the studios on a regular basis, so the intervals between these auditions became longer, and eventually the trips stopped. My curls grew out, and my hair was straight again.

Every night when she came home from work, Mattie brought me a present—a pack of gum, a top, a toy boat for the bathtub, something. My uncle Roy read the funny papers to me after dinner, and then he always had to go out somewhere.

"Roy won't be happy," my mother said, "until he breaks every heart in Los Angeles."

Mattie just laughed. Roy was about twenty-six then, two years younger than Mama, and he had a lot of girl friends, although he never brought any of them to the house. He suspected that Mattie and Mama would never consider any girl he brought home good enough for him. He was a handsome, dapper man, and I never saw him without a suit and tie, even on Sunday mornings at breakfast.

Then, almost overnight it seemed, everything changed.

My mother had to enter a T.B. sanatorium in Anaheim. She had an operation, and one of her lungs was collapsed. A few weeks later she died there. After she died, Joe took half of the silverware (even though there was an Old English letter "W" intaglioed on each piece), sold his garage, and moved back to New York. We never saw or heard from Joe again. We had a parrot named Polly, and Roy taught the parrot to say, "Where's Joe?" But a few weeks later, Roy left, too.

The new dial system was coming in, and Roy was transferred temporarily to San Diego to teach people down there how to use it. He met a "hello girl" and married her. Mattie was very upset about this marriage because the girl was a Catholic, but because my mother had also become a Catholic to marry Joe Cassidy in the church, Mattie never said anything to me about it until long after Mama had died. Catholics, she explained, were compulsory breeders, and she hated the idea of Roy being tied down with a large family. And she was right. By the time I was twelve, Roy had three children, two girls and a boy. But by then his wife had ballooned to two hundred pounds, and they didn't have any more children.

After the breakup of our extended family, Mattie and I left the big house in Topanga Canyon, and she rented an apartment in the Figueroa Arms, at 41st Drive and Figueroa Avenue in southwest L.A. She could no longer afford a full-time cook or maid to look after me while she worked all day, so I was sent to the McKinley Industrial School for Boys in Van Nuys. I was eight years old, and for the first three days I was there I cried without stopping. The magic number, Mattie told me, was ten. When I was ten, she said, I would be able to look after myself after school, but for the next two years I would just have to tough it out at McKinley.

I adjusted to life at McKinley because I had to, and it wasn't a bad place to be; it was just that two years seemed like a long time. The school, as I was told, was supported in part by the Kiwanis Club, and the parents of the boys who were placed there paid a prorated fee, depending upon their income. Mattie paid fifty dollars a month, but there was a long waiting list, and it had taken "pull," she said, to get me into the school.

There were more than two hundred boys there, ranging in age from six to eighteen, and we were separated by age into dormitories in four different two-story brick buildings. There was a matron in charge of each age group, and I was in Founders, Junior, with eight-year-olds. We had our own wash room, with showers and toilet stalls, and a small study-room library in addition to the dormitory. There was a Book of Knowledge set in the study, a dictionary, a complete set of Tom Swift books, and several books by Horatio Alger, Junior, from the "Tattered Tom" series. After I read a couple of Alger's novels, I realized I had it very good at McKinley compared to the orphans in New York Alger was writing about. These bootblacks and newsboys were on their own, out in the cold, and slept in alleys at night. When they got into trouble, a judge would sentence them to thirty days on Blackwell's Island, where they did hard labor, and then they would be turned out into the streets again. Sometimes, by luck, one of them would rescue some girl by stopping a runaway horse, and be rewarded with a good job by the girl's father, but the rest of these boys, without luck, were still on the streets. There were no dates mentioned in these Alger novels, so I didn't make the distinction between the 1860s and the 1920s. I thought the books described current conditions. The boys who read Alger truly appreciated McKinley, so I imagine that's why there were several of these novels placed in every study room.

McKinley had two hundred and fifty acres of farmland, and the school was more or less self-sufficient for many of its needs. All kinds of vegetables were grown, and we had our own dairy and pasteurization plant. There was a bull, too, with a ring in his nose, rabbits, chickens, and goats. We ate very well in the dining room and surplus farm products were sold in Van Nuys. In addition to attending school (we had our own grammar school, but the older boys were bused into Van Nuys High School), every boy had a regular daily job of some kind. As we grew older, we were given more responsible jobs. I started out as a scraper. I scraped the garbage off the plates in the kitchen after each meal, and then handed the plates to another boy who took them over to the dishwashers. Two years later, by the time I left, I was a rabbit keeper, responsible for the feeding and watering of a hutch of long-haired rabbits. I also dropped the bucks in with the does for breeding, according to the schedule I was given, but another boy butchered and skinned the rabbits. I was glad I left McKinley before getting his job, which would have been my next task. The top job at McKinley was taking care of the cows, breeding them to the bull, milking them, and working in the pasteurization plant. This privileged work was reserved for boys sixteen and older, and was much sought after because they could go to the dairy any time the supervisor wasn't around and fuck the calves. When a boy graduated from high school, or turned eighteen, he had to leave McKinley, but there was only a handful of boys sixteen and older.

My grandmother visited me every Sunday, riding the streetcar to downtown L.A. and then transferring to the Pacific Electric train at the Hill Street station, which had a line out to Van Nuys and the valley. When she got off at the McKinley stop, she had almost a mile to walk to the main gate of the school. This was an all-day round-trip, including the hours she spent with me, and it was years before I realized what a sacrifice she made each week to come and see me on her only day off.

Once a month, however, I was allowed to go home for a weekend. I would leave the school on Friday afternoon after classes let out, and then ride the big red train through open country into downtown L.A. At the Hill Street station, I would walk slowly down Hill toward the May Company, and more often than not I would run into Mattie coming up the street toward the station. If she was late getting off work, or if I was a little early, I would wait for her outside the Eighth Street employee exit. We would then eat dinner at Leighton's Cafeteria on Broadway. I almost always selected the same dinner: a breaded, fried pork chop; a cold artichoke with a saucer of mayonnaise; a wedge of watermelon or cantaloupe; and a piece of hot mince pie á la mode with vanilla ice cream. Inasmuch as Jell-O and junket were the desserts served most often at McKinley, I had lost my fondness for Jell-O and wanted a tastier dessert. I truly loved that basement cafeteria on

9

Broadway, which I thought served the best food in the entire world.

After dinner we went to the movies. Usually we went to the Paramount Theater, which only showed Paramount pictures, because of the stage show between film showings. There was at least one headliner, someone like Pinky Tomlin or Bill "Bojangles" Robinson, and an M.C. who cracked jokes. I didn't always understand the jokes, but I laughed anyway. I rarely asked for an explanation, and was on my best behavior during my weekend visits, afraid that if I became a nuisance in some way my monthly weekends might stop.

When "Dixie" was played during the movie, and it often was, my grandmother would nudge me in the ribs. We then applauded throughout the song. Quite often, indeed, most often, we were the only people in the audience applauding, but when Mattie clapped, so did I. I never questioned her about it. I knew vaguely that "Dixie" and Mississippi were connected in some way, and that was enough for me. Later on, when Mattie told me stories about her life in Mississippi and Louisiana, and informed me that we came from "family," I gathered that we were superior to the Los Angeles "louts," and that we had to set some kind of an example for others. Because I was told so often as a child that I was superior I began to believe it, and although I know now (now that I am an old fart) that it wasn't altogether true, the belief has served me well throughout my life. It made me more tolerant of others, who didn't have my family background, and allowed me to accomplish a good many things I probably wouldn't have attempted otherwise. There is still no doubt in my mind that Mattie was a superior person. She was the most intelligent woman I have ever known, even though she was living then in what she called "reduced circumstances." As near as I can determine, she was about forty-five or -six when I entered McKinley, but she looked much younger. She was five feet tall, exactly, and she had a trim figure because she was on her feet all day. She had an abundance of pale blonde hair, dark blue eyes, and very white skin. Her fingers were arthritic, however, with red swollen knuckles, and she had bulging bunions on both big toes. Sometimes she would carve away at the bunions in the evenings with a razor blade. I couldn't bear to watch this procedure, even though she said it didn't hurt to slice off a few layers.

I remember her mostly in black because all of the salesladies at the May Company wore black dresses with detachable white cuffs and collars. Mattie had a closet full of black silk dresses, and she wore gold-rimmed glasses with a pince nez, glasses that were secured by a gold spring chain on a black shiny button pinned to her dress. These were reading glasses, but there were always two little dents in her nose where they pinched her. Mattie's skin was smooth and soft, and I would frequently touch her face with the tips of my fingers, and stroke her face just to feel the softness of her cheeks. She walked in a wobbling way she had been taught at a finishing school she had attended in Princeton, Kentucky, when she was a girl. She held her head and neck stiffly erect as though she were balancing a book on her head. Her feet, turned out at a forty-five degree angle, walked an imaginary straight line. To get the hang of the walk, they had actually balanced a book on their heads, she told me.

Mattie started to smoke Chesterfields after my mother died, and she was an awkward smoker. She was supposed to exercise her fingers, because of the arthritis, and she did this by playing solitaire, dealing one game after another. With both hands occupied with the cards, she would let a cigarette dangle from one corner of her mouth, squinting an eye against the smoke. The ash would get longer and longer, but she almost always remembered to knock off the ash before it fell. Her doctor told her that sauerkraut juice was good for arthritis, and she usually had a glass of iced sauerkraut juice on the table when she played different variations of solitaire. The grimaces she made when she took a sip made me laugh, and she would, of course, laugh, too. She had a soft southern accent, but most people thought that it was English—not southern— and many people would ask her, when they met her for the first time, if she came from England.

After the Friday night movie, we would take the "E" streetcar to Santa Barbara and Figueroa, walk the two blocks home, and get to bed by eleven or eleven-thirty.

When I awoke on Saturday mornings, around nine, she would be gone, already at work, and I would put up the beds. There were two large rooms in the apartment, a living room and a dining room. Both rooms had glass double doors, and the pull-down double beds were behind the doors, one in the living room and one in the dining room. The doors folded back, and the beds could be pulled down easily, but first we had to move the furniture to make room for them. The living room was furnished with a heavy overstuffed couch and matching mohair chair, and the carpet was an expensive Oriental. There were standing lamps with beaded fringes on the shades, and a large cabinet radio we called the "console." The dining room carpet was blue and green with a geometric pattern of darker blue lines that was supposed to be a Frank Lloyd Wright design. We still had the large mahogany dining table from the house in Topanga Canyon, and the seven tall brocaded chairs that went with the table. Polly, however, when he got out of his cage from time to time, had torn strips of wood from the top of each chair. Mattie never said it was time to go to bed. She just said, "It's time to move the furniture."

I would make and put up the beds, move the furniture back into place, and then eat breakfast. Mattie had taught me how to fry eggs in bacon grease and how to use the toaster, and I always had a glass of milk with my breakfast. When we ate breakfast together and Mattie drank her morning coffee, I wanted coffee, too, but she said it would stunt my growth. I wasn't allowed to drink coffee until I was twelve years old.

At ten or ten-thirty I would catch the streetcar downtown. The May Company had a large rental library on the mezzanine, and outside the library there were soft leather chairs where a person could sit and read and look down on the main floor. I would check out two books on Mattie's library card and read on the mezzanine until noon, listening to the mysterious bell signals as they rang throughout the store. The store bells were a code, Mattie told me, but only the floor walkers were told what they meant. I read a lot of books on that mezzanine, beginning with the Tarzan and Mars novels by Edgar Rice Burroughs, and, later on, after I left McKinley and lived at home again, the racier novels of Viña Delmar, Donald Henderson Clarke, and Tiffany Thayer. The public libraries did not stock these authors, and if it hadn't been for the May Company rental library, I wouldn't have learned much of anything about sex, except, of course, for the usual misinformation I picked up from the other boys my age at McKinley. One thing I learned at McKinley: there were perverts in Los Angeles called "fruits," and they would do terrible things to a boy if they could catch a kid alone. But inasmuch as all fruits wore red neckties, they were easy to spot and avoid. I saw a good many of these fruits in downtown L.A., and I gave them a wide berth.

At noon I met Mattie in the May Company tea room.

We ate tuna fish sandwiches with Coca Colas, and then she gave me a quarter before returning to the French Room.

After lunch I walked across the street to the Tower Theater and watched a double-feature. There was an orange juice stand on the corner of Eighth and Broadway, and you could drink all of the orange juice you wanted for a dime. But there was a trick to it, and I was cheated out of a dime several times until I finally caught on. The orange juice they pumped up was so astonishingly cold the first sip gave you a headache right between the eyes, and it was difficult to finish one glass, let alone two. The movie was a dime, too, and I usually spent my remaining nickel on a candy bar. I saw *One-Way Passage* with William Powell and Kay Francis in the Tower Theater, and the ending was so tragic it almost broke my heart. *One-Way Passage* is still my all-time favorite movie, but I have never risked seeing it again. I cried so hard when the movie ended the usher took me out to the lobby and gave me a glass of water.

At five-thirty I would go up to the French Room and, still carrying my books, would talk to the other salesladies in the millinery department while I waited for Mattie. These middle-aged ladies, all in black, all of them smiling, would make over me and kiss me and tell me how much I had grown since the last time they had seen me.

We would then ride the streetcar home, and Mattie would look at my books on the way. Sometimes she would ask if the books I had checked out were a little old for me, but she never censored my reading. I would finish the books before returning to McKinley on Sunday afternoon, and Mattie took the books back to the library on Monday, paying the three cents per day fee.

On the way home we would shop at Smith's Supermarket, at 45th Street and Figueroa. The supermarket was a new concept, and Smith's had been built without doors because it stayed open twenty-four hours a day. There was nothing else like it at the time, and people came from all over southwest Los Angeles to shop at Smith's. Mattie would then cook dinner while I listened to the radio and read in the living room. We always had a big dinner, and we used the good china and silverware. I would set the table, as she had taught me, including the salad and oyster forks, even though we had fairly simple meals. I liked pork chops, and chicken and dumplings, so we usually had one or the other; biscuits, which Mattie made from scratch; string beans or creamed peas; a small salad; and pound cake and ice cream for dessert. Neither one of us cared much for salads, but we always ate one before our main course because, as she said, we needed the "roughage." It was several years before I found out what she meant by "roughage."

On Saturday nights when I wasn't home, Mattie either went to a dance downtown with one of her lady friends, or she went back downtown to play auction bridge at a twentieth of a cent a point at a hotel on Spring Street. But when I was home for the weekend she stayed there with me. She would wash her hair, using Marchand's Golden Hair Rinse, curl it with an iron heated on the gas burner in the kitchen, and do other small chores she had put off during the week. Sometimes Marie Weller, Mattie's best friend, would come over. Marie had escaped from the May Company's French Room and had opened her own millinery store in Hollywood, which she called Maison Marie's. They would talk about hats, and rehash some of the arguments they had had with Miss Gilbert, the tyrannical buyer at the May Company. They always referred to the buyer as Miss Gilbert, and I got the impression that this formidable woman, who went to Paris and New York on buying trips every year, was about eighty years old. Later on, when I finally met Miss Gilbert, I was astonished to discover that she was only about thirty-five, if that. Marie was interested in designing, and they talked interminably about hats. Mattie, of course, was an authority, and sometimes when we were out she would point out a woman and tell me how much the woman's hat had cost.

"There," she said, "is a five-dollar number. Common."

Things were either common or uncommon with Mattie. I learned gradually what was common and what was not. Common was something to be avoided, and good taste could be learned. Money had nothing to do with commonness because a person could be poor and still have good taste and good manners. A woman with manners always wore a hat and gloves on the street, and never smoked outside her home. Mattie never left the apartment, even for a dash across the street to the drugstore, without putting on her gloves and a hat. The lowest priced hats in the French Room were fifty dollars, and they were all "originals." Mattie got a commission on each hat she sold, as well as a salary. Mattie's hats were designed in the work room there, too, and when she saw one of her hats duplicated (the downtown Bullock's, she claimed, would steal the French Room ideas, and copy the hats in cheaper materials), she would either discard it or have it made over in the work room. Mattie had a lot of famous customers and one day, when she had stayed home from work with a cold, Norma Shearer, the movie actress, called her at home and asked how she was feeling. Mattie was pleased by the telephone call and told me that Miss Shearer was a "real lady," whereas some of the movie stars she waited on were "common as dirt." She also sold a hat to Mrs.

Edgar Rice Burroughs, a large, overweight woman, and she told me about it because she knew how much I liked the Tarzan novels. But I was bewildered by this information at the time. I had thought that writers lived all alone in a room writing all the time, and it had never occurred to me that a writer would have a wife, children, and lead an outwardly normal life.

Mattie liked to sleep late on Sunday morning, but I was used to getting up early in the dormitory at McKinley. I would wake early and read until she got up at eleven, trying to finish my books so she could take them back to the store on Monday. I always told her I had finished them anyway, whether I had or not, because I didn't want her to keep them out for another month at three cents a day. As a consequence, I never learned how Viña Delmar's *Bad Girl* came out, but the title more or less gave it away. The heroine had to decide whether to sleep with her fiancé before they got married, and I am sure that she did, or the novel would have been called *Good Girl.*

When the time came to leave, around three-thirty, we always had the same argument. Mattie always wanted to ride the streetcar downtown with me to the P.E. station, but I didn't want her to go with me because she would just have to turn around and come back home again. At last she would compromise, and walk to Santa Barbara Avenue with me, and wait until I got on the streetcar. If I cried, she cried, too, so I learned how to hold it in until after I got on the streetcar. Parting was an ordeal for both of us, whether I left for McKinley from home, or whether she left McKinley after one of her Sunday visits. As a consequence, I learned later in life never to say good-bye to anyone. As an adult, I have never said good-bye. I have left wives and lovers, naturally, but I have always disappeared without a word. I am one of those men who leaves the house ostensibly to get a package of cigarettes, and is never heard from again. That way, it is easier on both parties. As long as a man leaves everything behind, including his money, possessions, and clothes, he will have no regrets when he begins a new life somewhere else.

When a boy is eight or nine years old, and an orphan, and all he has is a grandmother standing between him and his own demise, it is not unreasonable for this boy to think that this old lady of forty-five or -six will die before he sees her again. So each weekend, when I left Mattie at the corner, or when she left me at McKinley, I knew in my heart that she would die before I saw her again. For a boy of eight or nine, this kind of thinking is not irrational.

2

Mattie kept her word. In January, 1929, shortly after my tenth birthday, she took me out of McKinley, and I moved in with her at the Figueroa Arms. I had learned a great deal at McKinley, much more than I had realized. This became quite obvious after I met some of the other kids my age in the neighborhood. For one thing, I had learned how to play the harmonica, and had been a member of the McKinley Harmonica Band. There were about thirty boys in the band, and we had played at various Kiwanis and other club meetings in the valley. We always began with the "Lindbergh March," a stirring song for a harmonica band, and ended our concert with "My Wild Irish Rose."

During summer vacations at McKinley, when school was out, we worked half-days, either in the morning or afternoon, picking and planting vegetables. I had learned how to cut asparagus, using a knife with a black mark on the blade, how to pick pole beans and dig for potatoes, and I knew something about animal husbandry. The two years at McKinley had made me self-reliant, and I could do my tasks without supervision, knowing that the work would be checked later. My teeth were in good shape because we were forced to see the dentist on a regular basis. I was no longer a finicky eater, and would eat anything that was put on my plate. If you didn't eat everything on your plate at McKinley, the matron, who sat with us, would not let you have any dessert. I was much more sophisticated than the other children at Menlo Avenue Grammar School, where I enrolled, a few blocks away from our apartment house, but I was prudent enough to keep the things I had learned at McKinley to myself. This was an all-white, middle-class neighborhood, and the children at Menlo Avenue had been well-shielded from the reality of the world. Nevertheless, I made friends with the other kids on my block (41st Drive), and I played with them in the neighborhood after school.

I knew nothing about girls, however, because I hadn't talked to a girl my age for two years. I was curious about what a vagina looked like. I had read about them, and I understood the coupling process from discussions at McKinley and by observing the animals, but I had never seen a vagina. There was a girl my age on the block named Thelma, and sometimes we walked to school together. One day, after school, I talked Thelma into giving me a look. The dimpled recess looked small to me, and I asked her how deep it went. She didn't know, but she got a ruler from her father's desk and we measured it. It was only two inches deep, and she was as upset about the depth as I was because it was obvious that there wasn't enough room in there for my member. We both concluded that it would deepen as she got older, but this in-depth examination put me off trying to have any sexual relations with a girl until I was thirteen years old.

The next two years were the happiest in my life. I had Mattie all to myself, and all of Exposition Park, a few blocks away, as a playground. After school I would change from school clothes into coveralls, as we had at McKinley, and either play on the block or walk over to Exposition Park. At six P.M., I would meet Mattie at the corner of Figueroa and Santa Barbara when she came home from work. Sometimes, when she didn't feel like cooking dinner, we ate at the drugstore on the corner. At other times, she cooked dinner and I would help her with the dishes and cleaning up. My only major complaint, which Mattie ignored, concerned the black knickers and black knee socks I had to wear. Los Angeles was not Greenville, Mississippi, but Mattie never acknowledged the difference. All of the other boys my age and older wore long trousers, either in corduroy or cotton, and we all wore shirts and ties to school. But I was the only kid in the school who wore knickers. Mattie couldn't even find any knickers in Los Angeles. She had to send to Greenville for them, where my Aunt Lilly, who had married Mattie's older brother, Crit Lowey, still lived. Aunt Lilly would mail out the knickers, and I had to wear them until I was twelve years old. Twelve was Mattie's rule for changing into long pants. I had learned how to fight at McKinley, and when someone at school jeered at me about the knickers I would wait until I caught the kid alone in the boys' room, and then I would punch him in the stomach. Sometimes, I would lay in wait for the boy after school, and then jump out from behind a hedge and sucker punch him in the stomach. Because there were no witnesses to these fights, I never got into any trouble about them. I had learned at McKinley that the boy who throws the first punch, instead of standing around arguing, invariably wins the fight. I had also learned that to avoid hurting your hand, it was best to hit your opponent in the stomach—not the head. But I hated the knickers, and I was always happy to get home after school and change into my coveralls with long legs.

I trusted Mattie to tell me the truth about things, and she always did, but her values were different from the Angelenos', and some of the things she told me didn't hold true for Los Angeles. She told me I should always be polite to colored people, and if they were old to address them as "Uncle" and "Auntie." A few months later I got a job selling the *Los Angeles Daily News* on the corner at Santa Barbara and Figueroa. The tabloid sold for two cents, and I got to keep a penny. One morning I said to an elderly Negro man, "Would you like a paper, Uncle?"

The man became enraged. "Don't you 'Uncle' me, you little prick!" He tried to kick me, but I dodged his foot and ran down the block. I waited down the block until he got on the streetcar before I returned to the corner. An L.A. Negro was not the same as a Mississippi or a Louisiana Negro. I have never made the mistake of addressing a black person as "Uncle" or "Auntie" again. But Mattie was a product of her environment, just as I was—or was becoming—a product of mine. There were certain things she *knew* that were no longer true, even though they may have been valid when she had learned them.

Our apartment was on the ground floor, with the two dining room windows facing Figueroa. Figueroa Avenue was the main artery to Long Beach, and the traffic noises were loud day and night. We became accustomed to the noise, but at night Mattie closed the windows. She thought that night air caused malaria.

"Night air carries miasma," she said, "and miasma carries malaria."

Mattie was also a firm believer in inherited characteristics. She thought that I would eventually be able to play the piano well because my mother had been an accomplished pianist before I was born. She still had Mama's Story & Clark upright against the dining room wall, waiting for me to start playing it. But I wasn't interested in the instrument and never fooled around with it. But I had supposedly inherited my mother's "ear," and perfect pitch, so that explained why I could sing so well and play the harmonica without being able to read music.

My father, who had died from tuberculosis when I was two (my mother caught it from him), had been a sales manager for Whitman's chocolates. His territory, when he had died, had been the four western states. Mattie claimed that my father could "talk a bird out of a tree," so I had inherited his "gift of gab." He had moved to Los Angeles from his southern territory because of his disease. Mattie blamed him for my mother's death because he had T.B. when he married her but had failed to mention it.

"But if he had told her," I said, "Mama wouldnt've married him, and I wouldn't've been born. Either that, or she would've married Joe Cassidy, and I would've been a Catholic instead of a Protestant."

When I would make a stupid remark like that, Mattie would just smile and accuse me of "reading Blackstone" again. I didn't know what she meant by "Blackstone," and when I looked for his name in the card catalogue at the Junípero Serra branch library, I couldn't find any books under that name. I discovered, years later, what she meant, but the name still has a sinister ring to it.

Mattie's father, my great-grandfather, undoubtedly read Blackstone. When she was a girl, he had been a judge in Princeton, Kentucky, and then, later on, the mayor of the town. He had been a lawyer first, and he won most of his cases, but when he won a case, Mattie said, he would take all of the spectators in the courtroom across the street to the saloon and buy them whiskey to celebrate his victory. Her mother had, as a consequence, made him run for judge so she would have a steady paycheck instead of trying to live on what was left of his fees after most of the money had been spent in the saloon.

After his death, Mattie had moved to Greenville, Mississippi, with her mother and two older brothers, Jake and Crit. Her mother died in Greenville. Jake had established a copper shop, specializing in construction work. Copper gutters for new houses were standard at the time, and he made a great deal of money. Crit Lowey opened a grocery store in Greenville. Later on, he had a stroke, and when he died, my Aunt Lilly inherited the store, which she continued to run by herself. Both of Mattie's brothers had been grown men when she was born, and they took care of her after her mother died. They both married Greenville girls. Her brothers were overprotective of Mattie, however.

Ed Sawyers, an electrical engineer, moved to Greenville from Kentucky, and opened the first electric light plant in the city. He was forty years old, and he fell in love with Mattie, even though she was just sixteen. Jake and Crit refused to let him marry her, but the couple eloped and stayed in New Orleans until Mattie became pregnant with my mother. Jake and Crit had searched for the newlyweds, but couldn't find them to annul the marriage. After she became pregnant there was nothing they could do, so Ed and Mattie returned to Greenville.

Ed Sawyers had a good thing going with his electric light plant because everyone wanted electricity. He made a handsome profit by including a twenty-percent mark-up for himself on every bill. The city fathers finally bought the plant from him to reduce the city's bills, but they then had to hire him to manage it because no one else in the city knew how. The first Christmas he had the plant, he had bulbs painted in various colors, and then had them strung up on a giant pine in front of the plant. When he lit the tree on Christmas Eve, farmers came in wagons from as far as forty miles away to take a look at it. No one had ever seen anything like it, and his lighted Christmas tree made him famous in Mississippi.

By the time she was nineteen, Mattie had two children: Mama and Roy. Before she could get pregnant again, a man came into Ed's office at the plant and killed him with a shotgun while he was seated behind his desk. The man claimed that Ed had had an affair with his wife, so he wasn't tried for the murder. But Mattie never believed the man. He was let off, she claimed, because people in Greenville had it in for my grandfather. He was a stranger who had come into town and made a lot of money, and the towns-people resented it.

Mattie sold the house in Greenville, and bought a hotel in Ruston, Louisiana, with the insurance money. She did a good business with the drummers who came into Ruston, and she also played cribbage after dinner with these traveling salesmen. She played them double or nothing for their room rentals. If they lost they paid double for their rooms; if they won, they had a free room for the night.

24

This was a foolproof system for Mattie. She was an excellent cribbage player, winning more often than she lost, and when she did lose she merely lost the income from a single room, not cash. She also sold insurance policies on the side and when she made a business trip to Little Rock or New Orleans, she would sell two or three policies to passengers on the train which would more than take care of her travel expenses.

The black employees in her hotel called her "Little Miss" because she was so tiny. The planter she was engaged to for several years in Ruston could span her narrow waist with his hands, she said.

I asked her once why she had never married again, but she said she didn't want to have any more children, and a man wanted children when he got married. She decided to wait until after she had a "change in life," but by the time her life did change she no longer wanted to get married. By then she was too independent. It never occurred to me at the time that Mattie and this planter she was engaged to for so many years might have been lovers, but I suspect now that they were. She was beautiful in her late forties, but in her early twenties she must have been ravishing.

One story she told me several times about the planter was about the run on the bank. The planter was a bank trustee, and one night he called her at three A.M.

"When the bank opens," he said, "take out all of your money."

"Why?" she said.

"Just do it," he whispered, and hung up.

When the bank opened, Mattie was the first customer. The bank manager didn't want to let her take her money out at first, but she insisted, closed her account, and got every cent. An hour later the bank closed, and she was the only person in town who got her money out of the bank failure. Not even her planter friend got his money.

"But if he knew something," I said, "why didn't he take his money out, too?"

"People would've known then that he gave me the tip. He still had his plantation, but all I had was the mortgaged hotel, and if I'd lost my money I would've lost the hotel. Besides, he was a gentleman, and I was a widow with two children."

Dinner was served family style at the hotel, with all of the guests sitting at one large table. Jake Lowey, her oldest brother, visited her occasionally, and once there was a lady staying at the hotel with slim ankles. She was proud of her ankles, and wore a wristwatch on her left one which she would glance at once in awhile to show off. One night at dinner an alarm clock went off. Jake had strapped an alarm clock around his ankle, and had set it to ring during dinner. He pulled up his trouser leg and shut off the alarm. The lady became so angry when everybody at the table laughed that she checked out of the hotel and caught the next train for New Orleans.

Jake's left eye was glass. He had lost his eye in a boyhood fight in Kentucky. He had the white desk clerk tell the Negro porter that both of his eyes were glass. The porter was skeptical, but Jake and the clerk had the joke set up for the porter to watch through Jake's bedroom keyhole when he went to bed. Jake had an extra glass eye, and he always kept his eye in a glass of water on his bedside table at night. When he went to bed that night, he took out the glass eye, pretended to take out the other one, and then groped his way to the bed. He then dropped both glass eyes into the glass of water and crawled into bed. The porter told everyone in town that Jake had two glass eyes, and he would get angry when no one would believe him. He knew what he had seen, and no one could tell him any different.

"Jake," Mattie said, "was a caution. I was always glad to see him come, but I was even happier when he left."

Jake made people apprehensive. He carried a pistol in his belt, and he had shot several men with it through the years. When he played poker with the drummers he would use his pistol as a weight to hold his money down. This was Jake's way, Mattie said, of keeping the poker game friendly and honest. He won and lost large sums of money playing poker in Memphis and on the Mississippi riverboats.

These stories, which I have barely outlined here, were told at great length, and with many details. Mattie recalled what people were wearing, their names, the precise time of day or night, what was served at the table, the expressions on the faces of the people concerned, the exact dialogue, and nothing was ever left out when she retold the same stories. There were dramatic pauses for effect, and when a tear was called for it would appear on cue, and Mattie, overcome with emotion, would wipe it away, shake her head, and continue. She told and retold the stories verbatim, and I always knew precisely when a tear would appear. I never tired of these stories, no matter how often they were told.

When her husband was shot, for example, there was a long delay before the sheriff came to the house to tell her about it. My grandfather was late for dinner, but when she called the plant and no one answered, she fed the babies and put them to bed. The cook, who was also Roy's wet nurse, went home. Mattie had something she called a "bone felon" in her right forefinger, and her finger throbbed and burned as though it were on fire. She couldn't sit still and she couldn't lie down, it hurt so much, and as time passed she worried about her husband as she paced the veranda. Finally, the sheriff, who had stopped on the way over to the house to pick up her doctor, arrived at the house. The sheriff told her that her husband was dead, and then the doctor lanced her finger. The doctor hadn't known about the bone felon, but had accompanied the sheriff in case she became hysterical so he could give her a sedative. But the relief she felt when her finger was lanced was so great she took the news of her husband's murder calmly. The import didn't sink in until the following day. It was more than a week after the funeral before she got around to crying. As a consequence of her initial reaction, which people considered cold, she hadn't gotten much sympathy from the Methodist minister or the other members of the church. But their reaction was fortuitous, she realized later, because it strengthened her resolve to go into business for herself, and not to depend on the help of anyone in Greenville.

Mattie had been successful enough with the hotel in Ruston to bring up her children and put Mama through college. Roy went to a business school in Little Rock, but took a job with Southern Bell before finishing his courses. Mama met my father in Jacksonville, Florida, when she visited a school friend there during summer vacation. My father, Mattie claimed, was a dandy. He traveled with a Negro valet and a steamer trunk full of clothes. He changed several times a day. He had white flannels for playing tennis, a suit for morning wear and another for the afternoons, and he invariably wore a dinner jacket in the evening.

"When he checked into hotels," I asked, "where did his valet sleep?"

Hotels at that time, she said, at least in the South, had basement rooms and separate dining rooms for the black servants of travelers. After my father moved from Little Rock to Los Angeles, and only worked part-time (because he was in and out of sanatoriums), he sent his black valet back to the family farm in North Carolina. Aileen, a senior in college when she met my father, had been swept off her feet by this glamorous, smooth-talking Tarheel. He came from an old family in Oxford, North Carolina, and had graduated from Chapel Hill, but a backward, agricultural state like North Carolina was too dull for him. To settle down on the family place like his two younger brothers would have bored him to death, Mattie said. He was a restless, ambitious man, and was always looking for a larger and richer territory. I had no recollection of him, of course, but I sometimes looked at his photograph, a studio portrait taken shortly before he died at the age of thirty. His recessed eyes stared straight ahead, and his face was pale and thin. He had a very high forehead, and would have been completely bald in another three or four years. Mattie said that he was handsome, but he did not look handsome to me in the photograph. His full lips were wide, and he reminded me of a shark. I did not want to look like him some day. I wished that there had been some other pictures of him, taken when he was younger and healthier, but there weren't. At one time there had been an album of snapshots, but after my mother remarried she had thrown the album away.

When my mother became pregnant, Mattie sold the hotel in Ruston and moved to Little Rock, Arkansas, to be with her. Roy went to work for Southern Bell. Then, after my father was transferred to Los Angeles from Little Rock, shortly after I was born, Mattie went along, too.

Roy also managed to transfer to the Los Angeles South-western Bell district, and we all lived together. Mattie didn't want my mother to live alone with a small child while my father was either on the road or staying in a sanatorium most of the time. Then, after he died, Mattie went to work for the May Company. Mama met and married Joe Cassidy.

But now there was just Mattie and me. For the next two years I had the most wonderful childhood any boy has ever had. In the summer, when school was out, I went to the Exposition Park playground every day. Sometimes I would play work-up softball all day long, from the time the park opened until it got too dark to see the ball. On other days, I went to the Los Angeles County Museum on the other side of the Coliseum. There was a children's museum in the basement, and tables with free paints and modeling clay. I could model in clay, or paint in water colors. I carved pigs and horses out of white bars of Ivory soap, and I painted one picture after another. I always made a tour of the art exhibits in the regular museum, too, spending a lot of time looking at my favorite paintings. I liked Dufy's water colors and Milton Avery's oil paintings best. One of Avery's paintings, a seaside scene, with ominous chocolate brown waves rolling in on a pink beach, fascinated me. One day the painting was no longer on the wall, and I mourned it like the loss of a friend.

I made dutiful tours of the mummies, looked at the World War display of weapons in the basement, and I was fond of the mastodon skeleton, but I much preferred the art galleries. I thought that I might become a painter some day, but I never have—not yet, anyway.

3

Shortly after my twelfth birthday, and not long after I got my bell-bottomed corduroy pants, my great uncle, Jake Lowey, and my cousin Ethel, Jake's daughter, arrived in Los Angeles. That was the end of my idyllic life with Mattie, although I didn't realize it at first. I was as happy to see them as Mattie was. But theirs was a permanent, not a temporary visit, and my delight in the new relatives soured in a hurry.

I loved my cousin Ethel from the first moment I saw her, but my Uncle Jake terrified me. Jake was twenty-four years older than Mattie, so he was about seventy-two or -three when he arrived in L.A. Jake's wife had been dead for many years, and Ethel was his only child. Jake didn't look his age because he held himself stiffly erect and there was a spring to his step. He was bald, with a freckled face and head, and the socket of his glass eye watered at all times. He would take his time about wiping his cheek with a sodden handkerchief. Perhaps at one time, the glass eye hadn't been so obvious, but as his eye sockets had recessed with advancing age, the bright staring blue eye no longer moved when the good eye did. And his good eye had faded, and didn't match the glass eye. Jake always wore a tie with a white shirt, but he never wore the same suit coat and trousers. I couldn't understand why he had three suits, and didn't wear them as suits instead of wearing the trousers to one and the jacket to one of the others. He wore black, high-top lace-up shoes like a policeman's, with white socks, and never went outside without his Panama hat. He carried a black ebony cane with a bronze dog's head handle, and the cane concealed a short three-edged sword inside. He wore a long-barreled .44 pistol in a holster on his belt, so he always kept his double-breasted jacket buttoned to conceal it. When he was outside, he would pause after every five or six steps, turn around completely (because of his one good eye), and take a long look before continuing down the street. He also smoked two packages of Granger rough-cut tobacco every day in his short black pipe.

Jake and Ethel arrived one night about ten P.M., after driving to Los Angeles from Lake Village, Arkansas, in Ethel's Model A Ford. I had to sleep in the living room pull-down bed with Uncle Jake, and Ethel slept with Mattie. It was several days before I learned about the circumstances of their sudden flight from Lake Village, but then Mattie told me about it in some detail when we were alone.

Jake had owned a small hotel in Lake Village, which he closed at night after the last Greyhound bus came through town at ten P.M. One night, after closing the hotel and going to bed, he heard noises downstairs in the lobby. He got his pistol, crept down the stairs from the second floor, and about halfway down the stairs, flipped on the lobby lights. Two burglars, with bandannas tied around the lower parts of their faces, were trying to open the safe behind the desk with a chisel and a hammer. When the lights came on they froze in place, and put up their hands. Jake shot both of them, and they were killed instantly with bullets through their hearts. As it turned out, the two thieves were only fourteen years old, and both came from respectable families in town. Jake was cleared by the sheriff, of course, but the feelings against him in town were, on the whole, unfavorable. No one denied Jake's legal right to kill the thieves, but on the other hand, the two boys had surrendered, and he could have held them for the sheriff instead of killing them.

Jake then heard rumors that the fathers of the two boys

he had killed planned to kill him in revenge. No attempts were made, however, because Jake, as a member of the local Klu Klux Klan, had a good many supporters in the Klan. But he knew that it would merely be a matter of time before he was ambushed some night. So Jake made a quick trip to Little Rock, negotiated the sale of his hotel, and left Lake Village with Ethel in the middle of the night after he got his money. The problem was, in 1931, he did not get the money the hotel was worth, although he probably could have gotten more if he had been able to wait a few months. He and Ethel arrived in Los Angeles with very little money to invest in a business of any kind. They weren't broke, and they owned the Model A Ford, but they didn't have much money. Jake would buy a bag of groceries occasionally, but he never offered Mattie any money toward the monthly thirty-five dollar rent of the apartment or for the utilities and phone.

Jake studied the classifieds every day, and finally bought a six-stool lunch room on Santa Barbara, adjacent to the Figueroa Theater's parking lot. The place was small enough for Jake to run by himself, with the help of a Negro dishwasher who stayed in the tiny kitchen. Jake served a daily luncheon and dinner special of beef stew, with cole slaw and a slice of white bread, for thirty-five cents. Coffee was a nickel extra. He also made ten-cent hamburgers on a grill, and every night after closing he baked three apple pies for the following day. But Jake's physical presence and personality were too forbidding to make a success out of a small lunch room, and there was very little walk-by traffic. He was open from ten A.M. to ten P.M., but sometimes three or four hours would pass by without a single customer. Across the street there was a drive-in restaurant under construction, which would be called "The Wich Stand" when it opened. Some of the construction workers would cross the street to eat at Jake's place, but most of them brought their own lunch and would just order coffee and pie. Jake would become furious with those men who just ordered a piece of pie.

"How can you work on pie?" he would ask. "Eat the beef stew, something that'll stick to your ribs!"

He would glare at them with his good eye, while the water would streak unappetizingly down his face from his glass eye. He wore his suit coat and odd trousers and Panama hat behind the counter, but never wore an apron. The beef stew he made was short on meat, heavy on the potatoes and carrots, and thickened with flour. The cole slaw was too pungent because he cut the mayonnaise with too much vinegar. He was also in competition with the drugstore's lunch counter, only fifty yards away, which served a daily blue plate special, different every day, including free coffee, for thirty-five cents. His apple pies were excellent, however, and several cops from the University Station often dropped by for coffee and a piece of pie.

After two months, Jake managed to unload the lunch room, selling it to an Italian who tried to turn it into a spaghetti restaurant, but he failed, too. In 1931, people were making their own spaghetti at home two or three times a week. The Italian, unable to find a buyer, boarded the place up. This was a bad year to open a small business.

Jake then found a job as a night watchman at a parking garage on Figueroa and 42nd Street. Because he had to stay there all night and sleep on a cot in the office, I got my bed back. I was grateful for that because sleeping with Jake had been an ordeal. Jake took a bath every Saturday night, and changed into a clean wool union suit, the kind that covered him from his ankles to his wrists, with a buttoned slit in the seat. But he didn't take the union suit off until the following Saturday night bath. By Wednesday, he was a little musty. I didn't know what kind of climate they had in Lake Village, Arkansas, but it was never cold enough in Los Angeles for long underwear. But because he was old, I supposed Jake was cold all the time. Either that, or he had gotten into the habit of wearing long underwear, and wasn't going to change a long-standing habit just because he had moved to southern California. He also slept with his loaded .44 pistol under his pillow. Sometimes, late at night, he would sit up straight in bed, clutching his pistol, and say, "What's that, Sonny? Did you hear that?"

What he heard, in all probability, was a car backfiring on Figueroa. But what he was worried about was the idea that the two men in Lake Village were coming for him, after tracking him to Los Angeles. He also thrashed about in his sleep, muttering, cursing, and belching up the lungfuls of air he swallowed. I would get as far over to my side of the bed as I could, afraid of disturbing him, and fearful that some night he would start blasting away with his pistol. So when he got the night watchman's job I was elated.

Mattie told me that Jake and Huey Long, the governor of Louisiana, were great friends. Every time Huey Long came to Lake Village, the two of them went fishing out on the lake. I believed her, of course, but I was bewildered by the information. Why, I wondered, would a state governor—or anyone else, for that matter—want to be Jake's friend? And why would the governor of Louisiana come to Arkansas to go fishing? If they were such good friends, I suggested to Mattie, why hadn't Jake gone to New Orleans instead of coming to L.A., where the governor could help him get started in a new business of some kind. But Mattie smiled enigmatically, and shook her head. There were a good many places Jake couldn't go back to, she said. New Orleans was one of them, and Houston, Texas, was another, but she never told me the reasons.

Jake took over the radio when he was in the apartment. He liked to listen to Father Coughlin, and to political broadcasts. He also admired Mr. Townsend, and the Townsend Plan that was going to give $400 a month to every Californian over sixty-five, with the provision that they had to spend the $400 before they got the next check.

"I can do that," he would say, lighting his pipe.

Jake sensed my fear of him, I am positive, though he would smile when I came in, and say, "Well, Sonny . . ." But we didn't have much to say to one another. One afternoon, however, he taught me how to play Red Dog, and how to deal seconds and cut the cards with only one hand.

Although I disliked Jake, I was crazy about Ethel. She was a vivacious woman in her early thirties. She had played the violin well enough to give recitals in Little Rock, but she also played our piano and sang. She faked a lot on the piano, playing by ear, although she could, of course, read music, and she had a strong walking left hand. She would play and both of us would sing after dinner, and she taught me how to sing the blues. Ethel wasn't pretty because she had enormous bubble brown eyes that were popped out with the whites showing all around. She had large breasts, but skinny legs. Mattie told me, privately, that Ethel reminded her of a drum on toothpicks. But this was an exaggeration; Ethel was slim, with a flat stomach. Her heavy breasts were disproportionate to her skinny arms and legs. When she imitated Fanny Brice, rolling her popping eyes, and throwing her long arms around, and standing on one leg as she sang, "My Man," she was truly funny.

Ethel had been married twice, and both of her husbands

had committed suicide. Her first husband had been a soph-omore when she was still a freshman at the University of Arkansas. She didn't know why he had killed himself, but after his death she left college, although she continued to study violin with a private teacher in Little Rock. Her second husband was ostensibly killed in a hunting accident, but she knew different. Two days after his death she got a letter with his suicide note in it. He had made his death look like an accident, Mattie told me, so that Ethel could collect the insurance. But she felt guilty about his death, even though it wasn't her fault, and she had shown his letter to the insurance company. The company was still willing to give her a portion of the money, but she wouldn't take it. Mattie told me that neither death was Ethel's fault, but that didn't stop Ethel from feeling responsible. Ethel had also been tried for manslaughter in Little Rock. She had run over a black man on a bicycle. He had pulled out in front of her unexpectedly at an intersection, and the judge dismissed the case as an unavoidable accident. These tragedies had made Ethel leery about dating again.

After a few weeks, Ethel found a job playing the piano and singing in a restaurant on Vermont Avenue, near Ver-non Street. She became quite popular. It was only part-time work, from six to ten in the evening, so I still got to see a lot of Ethel during the daytime. We would ride around in her Model A, laughing and talking, so she could get to know the city. A couple of times we drove down to Santa Monica, and went out on the pier. In the middle of the week, when business was slow, they let us in free to watch the marathon dancers, just to have some people in the stands. The contestants didn't dance; they merely walked as slowly as possible around the floor, hanging on to one another, and I thought it was boring. But Ethel considered it exciting because, as she said, they wouldn't allow anything like marathon dancing to take place back in Arkansas. The churches, she claimed, would never permit it.

It was inevitable in a job like Ethel's that she would attract admirers, because she sang request numbers when patrons in the restaurant fed the kitty on top of the piano. She would also accompany any patron, man or woman, who wanted to sing a song. At first, however, Ethel was reluctant to date anyone. She then dated a neon sign designer for a few weeks, but dropped him abruptly after getting into an argument with the man's mother, who thought that Ethel was too old to be dating her son. He phoned so often after she broke off with him that I was told to answer the phone at all times. If it was the designer, I told him Ethel wasn't home. In time, his calls stopped.

But then Ethel met a fellow who had a great deal of money. He was an oil man from Texas, divorced, with a teenaged daughter back in Lubbock. He drove a new Packard and lived in a large house in Santa Monica. He would come by the apartment and take Ethel out to dinner and then to the Cocoanut Grove to dance. He brought her flowers and candy, and he was, in Mattie's opinion, "a perfect gentleman." He was about forty-five, with curly gray hair, and he almost always wore a gray suit—sometimes with spats—with a white carnation in his buttonhole. He wore the carnation, he told me, out of respect for his mother, who had passed away a few years back. I had no reason to dislike the man, but I did in a way because I was a little jealous. He wanted to marry Ethel. Mattie urged her to do so, but Ethel was reluctant to marry again. She was afraid, she told Mattie, because he might kill himself. After all, her other two husbands had killed themselves, and he might do the same. And even though the suicides were not her fault, she felt that she might be attracted to men who wanted to end their lives early. Even the neon sign designer, she said, had threatened to kill himself when she dropped him. But Mattie told her to be practical. Ethel had a heart murmur, left over from a bout of rheumatic fever she had had as a girl, and she would never be able to support herself by holding down a regular forty-eight hour a week job. Sometimes, when her heart was acting up, she had to call the restaurant and cancel her evening's performance. The Texan didn't want to have any more children; he was an attractive man; and he would be a good provider. These discussions between Mattie and Ethel went on for several weeks. I would eavesdrop on their conversations from the living room while they sat at the dining table in the evening and drank coffee. Ethel did not ask Jake for his opinion, nor did she discuss the matter with him.

Then Ethel came up with a solution.

She told the Texan that she would marry him if he would sign a notarized statement that no matter what happened between them after they were married that he would not commit suicide. He was genuinely puzzled by the condition because Ethel hadn't told him that her other two husbands had killed themselves. He knew that she had been married before, but he thought that she was divorced, not widowed. Nevertheless, he went along with the plan, so she wrote out a statement in longhand, and he signed it and it was notarized by a real estate agent on Vermont Avenue.

The wedding was held in our apartment, and Mattie hired a Presbyterian minister through the classified ads to perform the ceremony. The Texan's father was still alive back in Lubbock, and he had other relatives as well, but none of them, including his daughter, came out to Los Angeles for the wedding. My uncle Roy and his wife came

39

with their children, and Uncle Jake, wearing the coat and pants to his best suit, gave Ethel away. There were flowers, and after the ceremony we had a turkey and a wedding cake in the dining room. Uncle Jake had a bottle of bootleg bourbon, and all of the males present, except for the minister and me, had a drink in the kitchen before and after the ceremony. They drank in the kitchen because they didn't want the minister to see them. Ethel and her bridegroom then left for the Mission Inn, in Riverside. This was a very popular destination for Los Angeles newlyweds, and Uncle Roy had taken his bride there for their honeymoon, as he mentioned about six different times after the ceremony.

Ethel moved into her husband's home in Santa Monica, and I thought that everything would return to normal again. And for awhile it did. Jake only came to the apartment occasionally now, to eat the lunch Mattie left for him in the refrigerator, and to take his Saturday night baths. He kept his clothes in the garage office. Pinball machines had started to become popular, and they were being installed at a rapid rate in restaurants and drugstores all over the city. With these early machines it was possible to win money instead of just winning free games. If your score was high enough, two, three, or even five nickels would drop into a box in the machine. The player could either use the nickels to play again, or pocket the winnings. Jake, however, had cut a strip from an aluminum ruler, the kind that winds up on spool, and rounded off one end of it. By inserting the thin flexible ruler into the coin slot he could trip any machine and play as often as he liked for nothing. During the daytime he had a regular route. He would visit different places and win money on the pinball machines to supplement his income from the night watchman's job. He got caught a couple of times, and was barred from those places, but he was slick and he got away with it most of the time because no one suspected that an old man with only one eye was cheating the pinball machines.

Then Mattie lost her job at the May Company. The Depression had caught up with designer hats, and very few women could afford to buy them. There were layoffs in the designers' room also, and I began to notice that a great number of women were walking around Los Angeles with no hats at all, designer or otherwise. Even downtown you could see hatless women shopping, and when they quit wearing hats, they stopped wearing gloves. Sometimes, on a Saturday, Mattie would be called in for the day, but she no longer received a commission on the hats she sold.

Uncle Jake lost his night watchman's job at the garage, and moved in with Ethel and her new husband in Santa Monica.

My uncle Roy then had to pay the rent and the utilities on our apartment. He also gave Mattie five dollars a week for a food allowance. Mattie cashed in her $1,000 burial policy for the money she had put into it, and she sold Polly, our parrot, to Miss Gilbert, the buyer. Miss Gilbert had wanted to buy the parrot for years, and she paid Mattie eighty dollars for it. It was a mean-spirited bird, and I was glad to see it go. The parrot never bit Mattie, but I had been bitten several times when I changed the newspaper in the bottom of the cage. The parrot was worth a lot more than eighty dollars because it spoke a good many words. It still said, "Where's Joe?" in a plaintive tone of voice, but it also said, "Give me a kiss," "Polly wants toast and coffee," "Pretty Polly," "Good morning," "Sonny!" and made a rumbling noise deep in its throat that was a fair imitation of the trucks on Figueroa rumbling down toward Long Beach early in the morning. Mattie had owned the bird for twelve years, and she truly missed him.

41

I was now attending John Adams Junior High School, at Thirtieth and Hill Streets. I got up at five A.M., and sold the *Daily News* every morning until seven-thirty. After I was checked out, I had to run about two miles to get to school, and I was often late for my first class. The price of the *Daily News* was raised to three cents, but I could still only keep one cent from the sale of a paper, and in two and a half hours on the corner I rarely made more than ten or eleven cents. Lunch at school was a ten-cent cardboard carton of beans or spaghetti, so I needed a dime every day to buy lunch. Then I got the idea to buy a package of Wings for a dime, and I sold the cigarettes for a penny apiece in the schoolyard during the lunch hour. I could sell all twenty cigarettes easily during the period, and my lunch problem was solved.

Ethel's husband committed suicide, shooting himself in the head with a .38 pistol. There had been reverses in the East Texas oil fields, and he had lost every cent he owned in a bad investment. The funeral ceremony was held in a funeral parlor in Santa Monica. His father, an aunt, and an older brother came out from Texas to attend the funeral (but not his daughter). They came on the train, the Sunset Limited, and stayed downtown at the Roslyn Hotel. They hired a limousine and a driver to drive them down to Santa Monica. My uncle Roy was there, but not my aunt, and I was there with Mattie, Uncle Jake, and Ethel. There was a Shriner, wearing a fez, too; he had a check for Ethel from the temple. Another gray-haired man, with a face the color of boiled ham, represented the Los Angeles Standard Club. The minister the funeral director had hired knew nothing about the dead man, so he gave an impersonal canned eulogy, rushing through it in a mumbling rumble. The tension in the funeral home chapel, with all of the empty chairs, was palpable.

The Texas relatives blamed Ethel for her husband's suicide, and none of them would speak to her. When the minister finished his eulogy, and slipped out the side door, Ethel whipped the signed affidavit out of her purse and tried to get the Texas relatives to read it. She was talking fast in her Arkansas drawl, trying to explain, but none of the relatives, including her husband's father, would look at the notarized statement. The Standard Club member took a drink from his flask, and the Shriner took off his fez and looked inside it, as if he were searching for an answer. Then Ethel started to read the affidavit aloud.

Mattie's lips began to twitch, and so did mine. We looked at each other, and then we ran out of the room. In the corridor, right outside the door, we could hold it in no longer. We began to laugh, and we laughed so hard I collapsed on the floor, and Mattie had to lean against the wall for support.

As I look back, I realize that that was the happiest moment of my life.

4

A year later my position became untenable. Uncle Roy couldn't support himself, a wife and three children, Mattie, and me, too. I left home and went on the road. I wasn't alone. For the next few years there were thousands of boys my age riding freight trains to nowhere. But no one can ever tell me I didn't have a happy childhood.

PART TWO

OPERA

1

I've been looking at the hats in my closet. My favorite is the insouciant straw Homburg I purchased in a superstud hat shop in Atlanta. I have only worn it twice in Miami; people down here look at you funny when you wear anything that hints at formality.

In Miami, they don't understand hats. Hats are for moderate or colder climates. A few years ago I was teaching a class on the contemporary world novel, and I was discussing Samuel Beckett's trilogy, *Malone Dies, Molloy,* and *The Unnameable.* I did a fifty-minute hour on Beckett's hats, and what they mean to him. Beckett truly understands hats, as well as he does pencil stubs, canes, crutches, bikes, and other neat objects that a man can use in self-defense. I was trying to get this business about hats over to this group of college students. But I never did. None of the members of the class wore a hat. Black students almost always wear some kind of hat even in class, but white college students, male or female, rarely wear hats in Miami. But black students, who understand hats very well, seldom, if ever, take college courses in the contemporary world novel. Black students prefer math, chemistry and physical education courses. The only courses blacks hate worse than English are philosophy courses.

But blacks know a lot about hats.

There is a good deal to know about hats, and nobody knows all there is to know about them. The important thing is to come to terms with hats in general, and then, if you are still up to it, you can examine your relationship, in depth, with one specific hat. That's what I am trying to do now: I want to close the relationship with a cowboy hat I had for a few minutes back in 1933. I have been putting it off for a long time. Every time the memory of this particular hat battles its way up through my subconscious, demanding that I take a closer look at it, I have pushed it back down again.

It was what they call a ten-gallon cowboy hat. This kind of hat will hold ten gallons of water, one gallon at a time, before it starts to leak through the crown; and a horse can drink out of the hat, one gallon at a time. In a few more years, when we eventually accept the metric system, it will probably be called a 37.5 liter hat, and then it will be so absurd that I will never be able to write about it. At this point, even after all of these years, I am still not sure I can write about it.

For foreground, I will return for a moment to the hats in my closet. The straw Homburg, the hat I mentioned in the first paragraph, was purchased in Atlanta on the day the shooting ended on my movie, *Cockfighter.* I don't know why I wanted the hat, but the important thing was that I could afford to buy it. It was twenty dollars, and I intended to deduct the cost from my income tax that year because I wore the hat to an interview with a reporter on the *Atlanta Journal Constitution* Sunday Magazine. As a rule I usually forget to deduct most of the things I am entitled to deduct because I forget to write them down at the time. But I kept the receipt for the hat, and if I am ever interviewed again by an Atlanta reporter I will wear it again. I would have deducted the lunch, too, but he (his paper) paid for that. So much for the straw Homburg. I put it on once in awhile, when I come across it in the closet, but I never wear it outside. This is a hat I am keeping for interviews with Atlanta reporters, and that is all.

There is a little story about each hat in the closet, very short little stories without much point to them, but that is because I am talking about hats in general, in the aggregate, this big bunch of hats in there, and I am trying to get them out of the closet.

There is a tennis hat in there, for example, with netting on both sides for ventilation. I no longer play tennis, but if I walked around all the time wearing this hat (powder blue, with white netting), people would think I was a tennis player.

"How's your backhand, Charles?"

"Still working on it," I could lie, with a shy smile.

I occasionally wear the tennis hat when I drive my car. At stop lights, I suppose, in the morning, other drivers look over at me and think, "There's a man going to play tennis," or, if it is late in the afternoon, "There's a man going home after ten sets of tennis." I undoubtedly get a lot of unearned credit as an athlete that way, just by wearing my tennis hat in the car.

But I don't play tennis. I quit playing tennis in 1939, after the girl I was engaged to beat me three love sets in a row. These humiliating sets were played in Exposition Park, at the public courts, in Los Angeles. After the last set I broke our engagement immediately, and I have never played tennis with anyone again. I have played some squash and handball, but not tennis. Even when I was a very young man I understood in a vague, or intuitive, way, how to cut my losses. If I had kept on playing tennis, you see, sooner or later I would have played tennis with a woman who would have *let* me win a few games during a set. My ex-fiancee, Edna May, was at least honest enough not to let me win a single game.

49

Sometimes, when I put my tennis hat on to drive to the supermarket a block away, I think about that girl, and about what my life would have been like if she had let me win a game or two in each set, and about what our married life would have been like.

I always conclude that it would have been hell, sheer, unmitigated hell.

Hats, you see, lead to these introspections, but when Edna May beat me those three love sets I wasn't wearing a hat. I was wearing a pair of blue corduroy pants, a black cowboy shirt with white pearl snap buttons, tennis shoes without socks, and I was playing with a borrowed tennis racquet and Edna May's balls. I was also unemployed, having just been discharged from the U.S. Regular Army. Perhaps, psychologically, I was beaten before I started to play, but I was playing to win. I tried truly, and when she kept acing those serves past me, again and again, I wanted to kill her. When the final set ended my shirt was sopping, and perspiration had run down my legs and into my shoes. There was a solitary drop of water on Edna May's nose, and she flicked it off with her left forefinger. I threw the borrowed racquet at her, but it went into the net instead of hitting her betweeen the eyes. I then left the court without a word. I never saw or talked with Edna May again. An abrupt break, I decided, would be the best thing for both of us. I was living with my grandmother, and Edna May called five different times. My grandmother tried to coax me into talking with Edna May, but I would not go to the phone. I had thought she might call once, or even twice, but I never expected five calls. For Edna May, that was a lot of calls. I wanted to talk to her every time she called, but I would not. She was a beautiful girl with blue-green eyes, and she wore her blonde hair long and in the same style that Pricilla Lane wore hers in the movie, *Four*

Daughters. Edna May's right breast was about a half-inch fuller than her left breast (she played a *lot* of tennis, and she was the intermediate women's champion of the Los Angeles Public Parks.) I still don't know what "intermediate" means in terms of tennis championships.

What I do know is, she didn't let me win a single game.

Another hat in my closet I like is the plaid deerstalker that Jean Ellen brought me back from England as a present. Jean Ellen was an English professor who quit teaching a few years ago to start a one-woman commune up in North Carolina. But when she bought me the deerstalker she was still deeply into the teaching of English and she had spent a summer vacation taking a course in eighteenth century English literature at the University of London. She thought the hat was an amusing gift for me. Perhaps it is, but it is all wool and much too warm to wear in Florida.

There are a good many other hats in the closet: two billed caps, a poplin and a soft wool English motoring cap; a blue felt hat, which I wore in a picture on a dust jacket once; a black Superfly hat with a studded leather hatband; two Panamas that I bought in Balboa, Panama, which were made in Ecuador; a "CAT" workman's cap; and a few assorted canvas and terrycloth hats suitable for wearing at the beach. Each one of these hats has a little story to go with it, too, but now I am ready to write about the cowboy hat and what happened to me because of it in 1933.

I know now that I can write about it because I was able to write about my break-up with Edna May. At one time, both in conversation and in writing, to avoid certain painful subjects, I would invoke the word "inchoate." But "inchoate" is a copout word.

Nothing is inchoate.

2

*T*he cowboy hat was on a nail on the back of the unpainted
door to the men's room. I didn't see it until I had entered and
closed the door. It was the archetype of all cowboy hats: the
cowboy hat. The color was a rich tobacco brown, although it
was encrusted with dirt and dust. The brim, about four inches
wide, was pinched in front to a nippled point. The sides were
curled into rakish arabesques—just enough, but not too much.
No one knows exactly why the side brims of a cowboy hat are
curled that way, although popular legend has it that the brims
are curled to enable three or four cowboys to ride comfortably in
the front seat of a pick-up truck. There was an inch-high
rattlesnake skin band, and there were jagged peak-and-valley
sweatmarks above the band. These glittering sweatmarks were
salty white against the dark tobacco brown. There was a hole
in the crown, a slightly ragged and circular hole large enough
to stick a finger in. A bullet hole? My heart thrilled at the
thought that it could be! There was also a leather thong that
was loose in front, encircling the crown, with the two ends
dropped down through two holes of the brim about midway
back from the front of the crown. The thong ends were long
enough to be tied beneath the wearer's chin. I took the hat down
from the nail and looked inside. It was a Stetson, size 7¼, and
the perforated sweatband was maculate with hair oil. A few
black curly hairs were caught in the sweatband. I tried it on,
but the hat was too big for me. I unrolled some toilet paper and
made four square pads, each one about an eighth of an inch
thick. When I placed these pads under the sweatband, the hat
fit my head beautifully. I tied the two loose ends of the thong
under my chin.

Then I took a piss, and tried to think of what I had to do . . .

3

In March, 1933, Pearson, Billy Tyson, and I sat on a slatted bench in Alligator Park, El Paso, Texas.

"I miss that nickel," Billy Tyson said, "and I wish I had me another one. The next guy that comes by I'm gonna ding him for a nickel."

"What nickel?" I said.

"The nickel I had about a week ago. I miss it, now that I ain't got it. Long's I had the nickel I felt pretty good, you know. I wasn't dead broke, but once I spent the nickel I felt loweren hell again."

"Why'd you spend it, then?"

"It was an accident. I bought me a candy bar with it, a Baby Ruth. And it was lucky I had the nickel, too, because I'd done taken three Baby Ruths already—they was in my shirt—when the man grabbed my hand. I was tryen for another one, you see. So I give him the nickel for the one he caught me with, and he was dumb enough to let me go without searchen me."

"If you got four Baby Ruths for a nickel," I said, "at least you got your money's worth."

"Maybe so, but I lost my nickel. I ain't tried to steal no candy bars since, or nothing else. If you don't have at least a nickel, or nothing, you just can't go in some store and look around. If they search you, and you don't have no money at all, they know damn well you're in there to steal something. Just to go on liven, a man needs at least a nickel in his pocket and I really miss that nickel."

Billy Tyson was not a man. He was fourteen years old. We were both the same age, although we both claimed that we were seventeen if we were asked how old we were.

Billy was from Harlan County, Kentucky, and he talked in a strange way. He didn't talk funny because of his Kentucky accent, although he had one of those, too, but because all of his side and back jaw teeth were missing. He had four upper front teeth and four lower front teeth, but no back teeth. None of the back teeth had ever grown in, he said, after he lost his baby teeth. Without any back teeth, ever, his jaw had narrowed as he had grown, and his tongue was too big for his mouth. So Billy talked funny, rapidly, and most of the time. A stranger would have difficulty understanding him, at least at first, but after you got used to his way of talking, he was as clear as anyone. Billy could eat almost anything, however. He broke up the big hunks with his eight front teeth, and then gummed the rest until he got it down to swallowing size. His gums, I thought, were probably as tough as saddle leather.

An elderly, fussy-looking man, with a little white Spitz on a leash, came down the gravel path. Billy got up from the bench.

"I'm gonna to ding that guy for a nickel."

"Pearson," I said, "d'you think that man'll give Billy a nickel?"

Pearson shrugged.

Billy talked more than I did, but I talked more than Pearson. Pearson rarely originated a conversation, but sometimes he could be drawn into one. He seldom answered irrelevant questions either, but that didn't stop Billy or me from asking them.

Billy Tyson was about two inches shorter than me. Pearson was about my height, but at first glance he looked shorter than Billy. That was because he was so bulky in his clothes. Without his clothes on he was a slight man of about 140 pounds. I weighed about 130, and Billy must have been around 120. Pearson was a black man, with skin the color of a dusty eggplant. He was somewhere between thirty-five and forty-five years old, and his bulky look was caused by all of the clothes he was wearing. He wore six shirts, one on top of the other, his suit coat (the pants to the suit were the second pair), and over the suitcoat he wore a brakeman's blue denim jacket. And over all of these clothes, he wore a long black Chesterfield overcoat with a velvet collar. He wore two caps: one made from a woman's stocking, with the top tied in a knot; over the stocking cap he wore a watchman's black knitted cap pulled down to his ears. Over the knit cap he wore a dirty gray Borsalino, with most of the fuzz worn off. His blue-black face was round enough to make his eyes squinty, and there were deep lines from the wings of his broad nose down to the corners of his mouth. His moustache and short goatee were mostly black, but there were a good many white hairs scattered about in his facial hair. Pearson's moon face, together with his bulky clothes, made him look like a well-fed middle-weight.

But Pearson wasn't well-fed. None of us was well-fed. It was now about seven P.M., and we hadn't had anything to eat since seven-thirty that morning, when we each had a bowl of vegetable stew, a slice of bread, and a cup of cocoa at the transient breadline down at the RR yards. There had been more than a hundred bums in the line, and not only were there no seconds, the men at the end of the line had missed out on the cocoa.

Billy and I were road kids. Pearson, although he didn't like the designation, had gradually acquired a bindle, which made him a bindle stiff whether he liked being called one or not. Pearson had a tattered army blanket rolled up in a canvas shelter-half, and inside the roll he carried a small frying pan, a spoon and a hunting knife, matches, an empty coffee can with wires attached so he could boil water in it, a sewing kit, and a few other small items. On the road a man had to make a decision rather early on, either to carry a bindle or to travel light. If a man had a bindle he could sleep a lot warmer in a boxcar, or at night in a jungle, but anyone who saw a man with a bindle knew, immediately, that here was a bum. If you were young enough, like Billy and me, and only carried the stuff you could cram into your pockets, people might pass you by, as you wandered about town, and think that you were simply a poor and dirty local kid. The idea was to be inconspicuous, to keep as clean as possible under the circumstances, and to avoid arrest. Trying to remain inconspicuous, and the fact that kids don't like to lug bulky things around with them, made Billy and me light travelers. Billy had been on the road for about six months, and I had been on the road about three. On the road, time doesn't mean a hell of a lot because a bum lives in the immediate present. Sometimes, a day can pass before a man notices it; at other times, a day can last forever—or at least seem that way.

Pearson had been on and off the road several times during his lifetime (I don't know how many), but he didn't consider himself as a professional bum or bindle stiff. His plan was to go to Detroit and get a job on the assembly line of some automobile plant. Pearson had a wife and a child in Chicago and he had another wife and a child in Los Angeles, he said. He wanted to get from El Paso to Detroit without passing through Chicago, and he could not, ever, he claimed, return to Los Angeles. When he got to Detroit and found a good job on the assembly line (he figured he would get one, eventually), he was not going to take up with a woman again, or have any more children.

Two wives and two children were enough for any man, he said, and he had finally learned his lesson.

My destination was Chicago, and the World's Fair. That, at least, was my tentative destination, but it still seemed as remote to me now as it had when I had left my home in Los Angeles. After three months on the road, going to Chicago was now just my cover story, a vague goal that I despaired of ever reaching. But when I was asked where I was going, the first question everybody always asks, I always said, "I'm going home to Chicago."

I had never been to Chicago, and I didn't know anyone there, but I had a cover story all prepared, including a mythical aunt with a flower shop, and there was also a job waiting for me on the midway at the World's Fair.

When I first hit the road, a bum in Colton, California, had told me that a man should always have a destination of some kind in his mind, even though he had no real plan and knew in his heart that he was going nowhere. There were literally thousands of new bums riding the freight trains in 1933, and very few of them had actual destinations. When they were asked where they were going, the standard answer was that they were looking for work. This answer, the professional bum told me, was much too indefinite for anyone in authority because authorities everywhere knew that there was no work anywhere. Not only, he said, did a man need a final destination, he had to add that he already had a job waiting for him when he got there. And somehow, he concluded, it was best for a man to actually believe that he did have a destination, and to head for it. He, he said, was going to New York, and he knew that he would make it, too, because he had been there before. When he got there, he planned to leave immediately, of course, and go to New Orleans, because he hated New York. But at least, having a destination in mind kept a man from thinking he was merely on an aimless journey to nowhere. What he said made a lot of jsense to me.

But even with my destination in mind, Chicago, I still felt that my traveling was aimless, because in three months I had only made it from Los Angeles to El Paso. It was still much too cold to continue farther north, so I had been riding back and forth from Yuma to Tucson, from Tucson to Douglas, and then back again. And when I traveled west instead of east I felt like a fool when I told someone I was going to Chicago. Each one of these cities was a division of the Southern Pacific Railroad, except for Douglas, which was a subdivision. The cities were all roughly two hundred miles apart, and it was a twelve or fourteen hour train ride between cities. From Douglas to El Paso was a long overnight ride, with a stopover either in Lordsburg or Rodeo, New Mexico. But the others were all daytime rides, hot and dry across the desert, and with monotonous, boring scenery.

I had been with Pearson and Billy Tyson for three days, and this was the first time since I had been on the road that I had traveled with anyone else. Until I had tied up with them I had been a loner, keeping to myself and, at jungle fires, hanging back on the edges of small groups, picking up lingo and folklore. I learned about RR schedules, which were important, but I also picked up a good deal of misinformation about almost everything. In addition to telling outright lies, most of the men I had met on the road were as full of misinformation as a black gambler at a dog track. But because I was young, and still somewhat gullible, I believed almost everything I heard until my own experience proved otherwise.

Pearson was my benefactor. He had outfitted me with

the clothes I wore, and I had more or less tagged along with him and Billy Tyson. And now, in Alligator Park (there were actually two immobile alligators in a small rock pit covered with chicken wire in the park), the three of us had been together for almost four days. But it seemed that we had been together much longer than that. My outlook about the road had improved considerably, and because I was now used to the companionship I wondered how I had managed to stick it out so long as a loner. I want to get on with Billy Tyson, and the cowboy hat, but first I had better go backwards.

I still don't know why it happened, but I know how it happened.

4

One dreary raining morning, instead of walking to school, I took the Number Five streetcar. When the streetcar reached my stop, at 30th and Main Street, it was still raining, Instead of getting off and walking a block in the rain to school, I stayed aboard the streetcar until we reached the Los Angeles River. By that time the rain had stopped. I climbed the low bluff to the park that overlooked the river and the RR yards below.

I could look down on the bums in the riverside jungle, and for awhile I watched the yard engines make up a train in the yards below. There were quite a few other bums in the park, as well as in the jungle, and I listened in on some conversations, asking a few questions of my own. The only time that bums were bothered by the law was when they first arrived by freight in Los Angeles. If they were leaving L.A. by freight train, the cops were glad to see them go, so catching a train out of the yards was a simple matter. Incoming trains were watched however, and the bums were rounded up frequently by cops as they detrained. They were then taken to Lincoln Heights Jail, given thirty days for vagrancy, with twenty-seven days suspended. They were told then that if they were caught hanging around L.A. again, they would be returned to Lincoln Heights to serve the remaining twenty-seven days. The word got around, of course, and the wiser incoming bums usually got off the train at Colton, a division point some fifty miles away, and made their way into Los Angeles by other means of transportation. But outgoing bums were not bothered by the RR bulls, and there were a good many bums hanging around the park and in the jungle waiting for an eastbound train.

The night I caught the eastbound freight, although I did not, at that time, have any destination in mind, I was wearing white socks and tennis shoes, a pair of corduroy pants, a white shirt with a blue-and-white striped necktie, and a gray roughneck sweater, the kind with a thick, stand-up collar. I also wore a gray baseball cap. I had a package of Dominos, a brand new dissecting kit I had stolen out of some U.S.C. student's car, and forty-seven cents in change.

The trip to Colton took a little more than two hours, arriving a little after midnight. In Colton, a division on the Southern Pacific, trains were made up and a helper engine was added to get the trains over the mountain to Redlands. Colton was only a few miles from San Bernardino, and was the loading and storage town for most of the fruit, oranges and plums shipped out of San Bernardino County, at that time the largest county in the United States. San Bernardino, or "Berdoo," as it is called by Californians, was the

60

whorehouse district for Southern California, with four square blocks of whorehouses, called collectively, "D" Street. At this time, Colton, California, in the winter, and Casper, Wyoming, in the summer, were the two major bum capitols in the United States. In the summer, Casper, with its miles of flat country and plentiful streams of water, was popular, but many professional bums wintered in Colton.

The open grassy fields outside the RR yards were ablaze with the lights of candles in the patchwork beanery tents; and at tiny fires, men slept on the ground like wheel spokes with their feet to the warmth. These open fields of the Colton jungle formed a transient Hooverville of more than 400 bums, although the population fluctuated daily. The jungle was cleared out periodically by the sheriff and a pick-up posse from town, but within a few days the jungle would fill up again. In Berdoo, about five walking miles away, there was a state-run transient camp which fed two meals a day, breakfast at ten A.M., and supper at four-thirty P.M. Many of the Colton jungle residents would walk over and back every day for one meal. There were plenty of oranges and plums to be had for nothing, because grove owners would frequently deliver free lugs of frost-touched oranges to the jungle. And in the prune plum orchards a few miles north of town, bums were allowed to pick up plums that had fallen from the trees. There were more than a dozen beaneries in the jungle. These were small businesses operated by owner-cooks. All that was needed was a make-shift shelter and a five gallon Standard Oil can bubbling over a wood or a coal fire and filled with either navy or kidney beans. There was usually a plank counter, with another plank bench facing the counter with seating for four or five customers, and a couple of bottles holding candles for illumination. A coffee can full of beans, with one thick slab of bread, was five cents. The beaneries were

61

busiest when a freight train came into the yards. It took about an hour to make up a train and to shift out a few cars, whether it was going east or west, and with a hundred or more bums to feed during that period, the owner-cooks had to work fast. Business was much slower between trains, and the entrepreneurs were not particularly competitive (although one beanery served hoecake, made with corn-meal, instead of serving white bread).

I hadn't had anything to eat since breakfast, so the beans I ate at midnight seemed perfect to me. The smoky interior of the beanery, a shack that had been constructed from flattened oil cans and canvas, was toasty warm after the cold wind that had chilled me on the train ride from L.A. After eating, I decided that it was too cold to continue on into the desert that night, riding in an empty gondola. I spent the next two days in the Colton jungle, hanging around the fires and picking up some useful information about the road.

On the third night, with a coffee can of water, and a gunny sack partially filled with oranges and plums, I caught the one A.M. freight to Yuma, Arizona. By ten A.M. the next morning, all of my water was gone. I had sucked the juice out of all my oranges, and I had a case of the runs from eating the plums. With my stomach cramping, I got off in Indio, and let the train continue without me.

I couldn't think of a single reason why anyone would want to live in a desert town like Indio. But it was a date shipping center, I suppose, with a mean living to be had, and that was probably why the town was founded. A bum rarely left the train at Indio. After begging for food at a dozen houses, I understood why. No one was hostile to me; if anything, they were merely embarrassed because they had no food to give me. Finally, a Mexican woman gave me three dry tortillas, and eating these helped to settle my stomach. I had given my leftover plums to a man on the train, after realizing that the plums were what had caused my discomfort.

I had squandered most of my money in the Colton beaneries, and I was down to eleven cents. At a gas station, a few blocks away from the yards, I traded my dissecting kit for a package of Wings. I then spent the next ten hours under a dusty pepper tree, smoking, dozing, and waiting for the next train to Yuma.

This was another night train. The weather was balmy, after a hot dry day in Indio, all of the way to Yuma. The stars were out, and I had a feeling on the train that I was getting somewhere, although all I managed to get to was Yuma.

At Niland, the last stop in California, where the train stopped briefly so the engine would take on water, grim men armed with ax handles lined both sides of the tracks to prevent anyone from leaving the train. They wanted to make certain that all of the bums stayed on the train and left California. On freights coming in to California, the bums were taken off the train at Niland and kept in a warehouse until the next freight came through for Arizona. So we had about fifty or more bums added to our train at Niland. They were hungry, although they had been given plenty of water in the warehouse where they had spent about eight or nine hours. The men with ax handles didn't meet every train that came through Niland, but they met enough of them to discourage many bums from trying to get through. To avoid Niland, some bums took a train from Phoenix to Prescott, and then tried to get a truck ride into California via Needles, but this method was difficult in other ways. A bum wasn't welcome on the train to Prescott, and if a man wasn't well-dressed, he could stand on the highway forever without getting a ride in a truck. Although, at the time, I didn't intend to return to California, and I had not as yet selected a definite destination, the realization that it would be difficult to get back into California through Niland made me feel as if I had passed a major milestone in establishing my freedom. I felt that I had, at last, truly gotten away.

I liked Yuma, as who would not? I have often wished that I could have spent the rest of my life there. But a tragedy forced me out of town, and I knew that I could never return to this wonderful desert city.

Compared with the glum expressions I had left in L.A., the Yuma residents I saw on the streets, as I explored the town on foot, wore almost childishly happy expressions. At one time, many years ago, Yuma had been a small sea port, with ocean-going vessels sailing up the Colorado to dock and trade there. But all that had been a long time ago, and now the river was shallow and narrow, with only the watermarks remaining on the steep bluffs to show how high the river had once been. The All-American Canal into California's Imperial Valley had helped to reduce the river's flow, as had the construction at Boulder Dam. There didn't seem to be any economical reasons whatsoever for Yuma's existence, at least that I could see, except that it was a water stop for trains passing through; and there was still a spur track that went down into some remote village in Mexico once a week. There were four Indian squaws squatting on the RR station platform. They sold crudely made pottery and turquoise beads, and could only have had minimal sales. The Sunset Limited stopped each way for only five minutes, and the passengers who got off the train were mostly those whose destination was Yuma. The Indian women didn't get up from their squatting positions to hawk their wares to the people on the train, so they only sold something to the occasional traveler who leaped off the train for a minute or so.

I passed a drugstore, and an Indian buck, wearing work clothes and a cowboy hat, stopped me on the sidewalk. I knew he was an Indian because he had two long braids of black hair down his back, and he didn't speak with a Spanish accent. He asked me if I wanted to make four-bits.

"Sure," I said.

"Here." He handed me a dollar bill. "Go into the drugstore, and buy me a bottle of rubbing alcohol. It's on the shelf, back by the pharmacist's slot, next to the shaving stuff. It's seventy-eight cents."

"Why me?" I was puzzled.

He shrugged, and spat into the gutter. "They don't sell Indians rubbing alcohol in Arizona."

I bought the rubbing alcohol for him without any trouble, and he let me keep the change, and made up the difference. I had only been in Yuma for an hour or so, and I was already making money. I did not, however, have much sympathy for the Indian. He looked as much like a Mexican as he did an Indian. If he had cut off his braids and faked a Spanish accent, he could have bought all of the alcohol he wanted without being questioned. Perhaps, I thought, he was too proud of being an Indian to fake deception, but wasn't it equally humiliating to have to pay some stranger on the street to buy the alcohol for him? To give him the benefit of my own doubts, I concluded that the idea had never occurred to him to change his appearance.

I then talked to another bum on the street, a middle-aged man, who told me that he was making a living as a professional witness. I was impressed by what he had to say. The wedding chapels in Yuma were open twenty-four hours a day and many California couples unwilling to wait the required three days would obtain a license, drive to Yuma, get married, and be on their way back in about ten minutes. This bum spent his nights hanging around all-night wedding parlors where he would be available to serve as a witness. He was tipped, he said, anywhere from a quarter to a dollar for watching the rapid-fire ceremony and signing the forms.

"In a way," he said, "I'm one of the highest paid men in Arizona. If a wedding lasts five minutes, and I get tipped a buck, I'm actually making twelve dollars an hour."

But too often, he added unhappily, three or four nights would go by without his getting a single witness job. This happened because a lot of couples brought friends along, and then got married with these friends serving as un-professional witnesses. He showed me his necktie, which he had curled into a ring and kept in a paper sack. "Some of these so-called friends of the bride and bridegroom don't even have a necktie to wear at the ceremony," he said bitterly. "And they're often drunk, and make crude jokes, like, 'Run for the door, Bill, and I'll hold her off. It ain't too late.' That sort of thing destroys the sanctity of the ceremony. But when they get me, they know they'll get a professional job."

The professional witness also told me about the deserted prison, and that it was available as a place to sleep, and the cops never bothered anyone who used it.

The ancient Arizona prison, abandoned at least fifty years before, was atop a gently sloping hill northwest of the RR station. There was a sandy road to the prison, and there were no other habitations nearby. The building was mostly adobe, and large sections of the roof had fallen in. Windows with bars were still in place at irregular intervals, high in the walls that were still standing, and sand had drifted in

66

where the high double doors had been at the entrance. The sandy floor was a soft place to sleep. The interior was unoccupied, but a good many bums had spent nights in the prison. There was some interesting graffiti to read on the walls, and the remains of fires and improvised cooking utensils were scattered about. I built a small camp fire, using some manzanita root someone had gathered, and set up housekeeping. I made a shallow bed in the sand by the fire, and covered it with loose straw. I picked a corner of the largest room, where a section of the roof was still intact and would be shady all day. I had bought a loaf of bread and a dime's worth of baloney in the grocery store, and after I made a stack of sandwiches, I settled down in my nest by the fire to eat the sandwiches and tried to think for the first time in my life.

Thinking, when you first try it, is very difficult. I had never tried to think before, seriously, I mean, and I didn't quite know how to go about the process. Most people, under ordinary circumstances, living with their families, attending school, getting jobs, don't get around to thinking until their early twenties—if then. Sometimes they are married and have two or three children before they begin to think about their lives. I have talked to men who told me that they never did any serious thinking about themselves until their mid-thirties. Thinking, as opposed to making rather superficial distinctions and decisions is, apparently, unnecessary for everyday life. Most people simply go along with their lives, accepting what happens to them, attributing to good and bad luck whatever fortune or plight comes their way.

But as I sat there alone, very alone, in the deserted and empty prison, with my mind alert for options—aware that there were options for the first time in my life—my mind reeled as I tried to get my thoughts into some kind of order. I was untrained in formal logic, and my mind kept going off on tangents. The experience was heady, exciting, bewildering, and I had to make a determined effort of will to prevent myself from being distracted by a buzzing fly, or even from contemplating the beauty of the swirling red-brown-ocherous pattern on a knot of manzanita root. It is much easier to slip into a daydream than it is to think.

Hours passed. But I was unaware of time as I tried to think things out. My thoughts were not profound, nor did they involve philosophy in any way. It was merely straight thinking, if that is the name for what I was doing, exploring ideas and possibilities in an effort to forge a new identity for myself. I was not concerned with any overall life plan, either for the immediate future or for the months and years ahead of me. The world itself would take care of my future, but what I needed for the immediate moment and survival was a believable background.

First of all, I needed a new name. My own name had been passed onto me by a man who knew that he was dying and who had wanted to have a small piece of immortality. Well, fuck him, I thought. The name would die with me, and I would never leave any abandoned children behind me when I died. And for the present, for security, I would choose a new name. If I were picked up for vagrancy, or if I went to jail for any reason, I could be traced by my real name, and I didn't want my grandmother to find out about any trouble I got into. It would be far better for her not to know about what had happened to me than it would be for her to find out that I was in jail somewhere, which everyone I had met on the road so far had claimed to be an ever-present possibility and daily hazard.

I decided to take my great-uncle's name, Jake Lowey. I liked the sound of it because it sounded much different when applied to me instead of to my ancient, one-eyed great-uncle. And perhaps, I thought, by using Jake's name, some of the old man's gift for survival would somehow be magically transferred to me.

I made up the name of an imaginary aunt in Chicago, imaginary street addresses for her flower shop and apartment, and I selected Chicago and the World's Fair as my ultimate destination. Also, when I was asked, as I knew I would be, I would say I had a job waiting for me at the Fair, working on the midway. As what? As a barker at a baseball and milk bottle concession. How come I could get a job so easily at The Fair, with everyone else wanting one? My aunt had influence with an alderman, and she had pulled a few strings for me, that's how.

I was skinny, but at five-nine I was tall for my age. My heart-shaped face was far too innocent looking to pass for twenty-one. And because I was a blond with a fair complexion, there wasn't even any peach fuzz on my face. But I could, I thought, pass myself off as seventeen going on eighteen when someone asked me how old I was; the important thing was to tough it out and stick with the lie. I worked out a new birthday, using a stick to do the arithmetic in the sand. I memorized my new name and birth date, saying them aloud, and casually, until they sounded natural to me.

As a birth place, I settled for Los Angeles, where many people live but very few are born, because, if queried, I could rattle off L.A. landmarks and street names. I knew the city well, all of it, and I could always say that my parents were dead, which they were. Ray and Aileen Lowey, deceased, and buried in Calvary.

I knew enough about Catholicism to pass myself off as a Roman Catholic, and this seemed like the best religion to choose because, if need be, I could probably get help at any one of the Catholic relief agencies in any city I happened to be passing through. I had learned already that it was a poor idea to admit to atheism, when I had told the registrar at John Adams Junior High School that I was an atheist. She had denied that I was an atheist, and asked me repeatedly to tell her my religion until I said, finally, that I was a Methodist—which I was not. On Sundays at McKinley, there had been interdenominational services, but they weren't mandatory, and I had never attended. My grandmother believed in God, or said she did, but didn't belong to any church. When I came home from McKinley, she had sent me to Sunday school a few times to the Presbyterian church a few blocks away from the apartment house, but the teacher, a young man with a lisp and a red necktie, was obviously a fruit. I withheld the dime she gave me each time for the offering, and quit going after a few weeks. But only adults were allowed to be atheists, apparently, so I decided that I would be a Catholic, if asked, at least until I became twenty-one.

I made up a good many new facts about myself while I was at it, such as high schools attended, hobbies and sports I had never engaged in, down to a made-up sexual experience with a second cousin. I then filed the imaginary details away in my head.

What I was doing, although it was many years later before I realized it, was manufacturing the basic background for a fictional character as a novelist must do in preparation before writing a novel. The novelist knows hundreds of small details about his major characters that he never puts down on paper, but the fact that he does "know" these things about his imaginary characters enables him to write about them with authority. I was never called upon to relate very many of the details I made up about Jake Lowey, but thinking about them and planning how to use them if needed strengthened my self-confidence. In fact, the seventeen-year-old Jake Lowey was a pretty tough kid.

That night, secure within my new self, I lay on the soft bed, watching the bright stars in the black sky, while, at the same time, moonrays slanted through the barred windows in the walls. I had a mixed and detached reaction to my new identity—retaining the old while stirring the new in random patterns in my mind.

The next morning I walked to the RR bridge that separated California from Arizona. I walked along the bluff, staying on the Arizona side, and finally found a trail down the cliffside to the Colorado River. I removed and washed my shirt and socks, and, while they dried, bathed myself with river water, using damp sand in lieu of soap to get off the worst of the ingrained train dirt from my elbows and ankles. I also cleaned under my foreskin, a habit I performed every day. A foreskin is a mixed blessing, advantageous in prolonging the sex act, but a hygiene problem that must be attended to every day. If a man misses cleaning under his foreskin for two or three days, his dick will become swollen and sore.

After an hour I began to get sunburned. I got dressed and climbed back up the trail.

Beneath a cottonwood tree, about a hundred yards away from the old prison, a man had pitched a pup tent while I had sojourned down by the river. He had a leather knapsack opened beside a small fire, and he was frying bacon in a small iron skillet. He wore a black suit, a white shirt with a maroon tie, and old-fashioned high-topped shoes that were well shined. He had a deeply lined and homely face, like that of a man who has lost a great deal of weight and the skin hasn't shrunk, as yet, to fit the smaller form within. He was in late middle-age, and his black hair was gray at the temples.

"Did you eat yet?" he said. This was the standard greeting on the road.

I shook my head, squatted on my heels, and inhaled the wonderful aroma of the frying bacon.

He cut two more slices from the slab of bacon he had in his knapsack, and after his slices were crisp he fried mine. While the bacon sizzled, he mixed corn meal and water in a tin cup, and when my bacon was done he removed it, added the corn meal mixture to the hot grease and made a hoecake. We ate the hoecake and the bacon without talking. He then cleaned the frying pan with sand before putting it back into the knapsack. He was neat, almost fussy, in his movements, and he didn't waste any motions. His long fingers trembled, however.

I offered him a Wing, which he refused, and I waited anxiously for him to ask me some questions. I was eager to try out my new identity on this generous stranger, but I wasn't going to volunteer any information. He remained silent while I smoked, and when I finished my cigarette and tossed the butt into the fire, he removed his suit coat, folded it neatly, and put it inside the tent. He then took a two-pronged metal whip out of his knapsack. The whip had been made from a wire coat hanger, with the wire unwound, looped over in the center, and the loop made into a handle, with adhesive tape wrapped around it. The two exposed ends were about three inches apart. It was a short but an effective whip.

"How'd you like to make fifty cents?" His voice was as trembly as his fingers.

"I don't know," I said uneasily, getting to my feet and preparing to run.

"All you've got to do," he said, "is hit me across the back with this thing a few times." He held out the whip, and got into a kneeling position.

"Give me the four-bits," I said.

"In advance?"

"Yeah. In advance."

Still kneeling, he fished two quarters out of his pants pocket, and handed me the money and the whip. I put the money away, and as he leaned forward, hugging his chest, I tapped his back gingerly.

"Harder!" he said.

I hit him a little harder, and as he kept saying, "Harder, harder," I increased the punishment, although I never hit him hard enough to really hurt him, or even to tear the fabric of his shirt. The two-pronged wire whip wasn't heavy enough to do much physical damage.

After awhile, and before my arm got tired, he said, "Thanks. That's enough."

I tossed the whip down beside him, and left for the prison. My stomach was churning from the experience, or perhaps from the greasy hoecake. Although I was delighted by the unexpected windfall of the half-dollar, I knew there was something wrong about what I had done. Something, I knew, was wrong about whipping a man for money. I hadn't liked doing it, and I had been frightened at first, thinking that I might hurt the man, but he hadn't flinched or whimpered. If he had yelled, or indicated in any way that he was in pain, I wouldn't have been able to continue. But inasmuch as it hadn't bothered him too much, I decided he was undergoing some kind of religious penance, like the flagellants in the Catholic church I had heard about.

That afternoon I went shopping in Yuma. I bought a package of Wings, and while I was at it I managed to steal a bar of soap, a candy bar, and a *College Humor* magazine. I returned to the prison, slipping by the sad looking man's little tent. He didn't greet me as I passed by, and I said nothing to him. I read the magazine until it got too dark, and then I went to sleep.

The next four days followed the same pattern. After I washed at the river (with the soap, I could now wash my hair), the man would cook and give me breakfast, pay me a half-dollar, and I would whip him with the improvised whip. On the fifth morning, after breakfast, he asked me to whip him for nothing. I considered it for a moment, and then I recalled the professional marriage ceremony witness I had met on my first day in Yuma.

"No," I said. "This is the sort of work I do for a living, and if it ever got around that I was passing out free whippings, I'd be out of business." I laughed, thinking that my remark was funny, but he did not join me.

"I thought," he said seriously, "that you might do it out of friendship."

That didn't go down well with me. "You aren't my friend," I said. "I don't know your name, and you've never asked me for mine. We've had a businesslike relationship from the first."

"But I don't have any more money," he said.

"I know what it is to be broke," I said. "My cousin Ethel sings a song that goes, 'If I ever get my hands on a dollar again,/ I'm gonna save it for my only friend.' But if you need some money, I'll lend you a half-dollar."

"Then," he said, "if I give it back to you, will you stroke me a few times with—"

"No." I shook my head. "But if you need the money for food I'll let you have it."

"Never mind." His face flushed with anger. He turned his back on me, and started to take down his tent, kicking the wooden stakes out with his feet. I watched him from the prison doorway as he rolled his tent and his blanket, and folded the roll in a U over his knapsack. Without once

74

looking in my direction, he started down the sandy road toward the RR station. I felt sympathy for the man, and I couldn't understand my reluctance to give the man a free whipping. But just as I knew that whipping him for money in the first place was wrong, I knew that to whip him for nothing would be much worse. There would be no end to it; it would be like Sindbad the Sailor and The Old Man of the Sea, in the story in *The Book of Knowledge* I had read at McKinley.

At any rate, I thought, when he was gone from sight, I now had a tidy little stake. Early the next morning, I caught the Pacific Fruit Express freight train for Tucson.

5

In the Tucson yards I talked to a Chicano who had just left the new state transient camp outside of the city. He told me all that he knew about it, and it seemed like a good place to stay for a few days. My lips were cracked, chapped and sore, and the long all-day ride across the desert on top of the reefer had sunburned my face.

"I been out there a month," he said, "but now I'm going out to Chico, California and pull sugar beets."

"You may not get through Niland." After I explained the set-up there, telling him about the men with ax handles, he decided to go to Prescott, and then blind a truck and get into California through Needles. Besides, Chico was in Northern California, and he would get there quicker that way.

The transient camp, the Chicano told me, was the first

of what was to become several camps, and it had been established by Arizona, with some additional federal money, to do something about the heavy transient population in the state. Not only was the camp system designed for homeless bums, it was administered by the transients themselves. Arizona had been forced to establish these camps because California wouldn't always let bums in, and they, the Arizonans, couldn't allow the hungry bums to ride trains back and forth through the state forever, or to roam the cities begging for food. Every bum in the camp, from the commandant down to the lowliest K.P. in the kitchen, was paid ninety cents a week in addition to receiving bed and board. The new camp resident didn't get on the weekly payroll, however, until he had undergone two weeks' probation.

After his two weeks of probation in pyramidal tents, he was assigned to a camp job of some kind, provided with a new set of clothes (work shoes, blue jeans, blue work shirt), and put on the payroll. He was also (at Tucson) moved from the tents into one of three wooden barracks.

These camps, to succeed, had to be strong on discipline. There was a small guard force of Camp Police, who were issued surplus Navy pea jackets, and armbands with C.P. on them. They guarded the main gate and the outer perimeters at night. A man could check out at any time, of course, so the professional bums, as well as the bums with somewhere to go, rarely stayed for more than three or four days. In three days, after a man has gotten cleaned up and has filled his stomach a few times, he's ready to go again.

"But some of these guys," the Chicano said, "have found theirself a home, and they'll probably sweat out the entire Depression out there."

As I discovered, the rules were considered strict, at least by the free-spirited bums, but the rules were not nearly as strict as McKinley's had been. The matrons at McKinley were always on the lookout for infractions, whereas the men in charge at the camps were fairly easy-going. If a man got drunk, he was kicked out of camp. If two men got into a fight, both of them were kicked out, regardless of who had started the fight in the first place. A man had to do everything the captain of his company told him to do or check out. Happily, there was very little to do, and we were never told to do much of anything. Most of the jobs, except for the guys who worked in the kitchen and mess hall, were "make-work" jobs, like picking up trash, or raking the yard and cleaning the barracks.

I bought two sacks of Bull Durham and picked up some free, extra packs of cigarette papers, and walked out to the camp, which was about three miles out of town.

I stayed in the Tucson camp for five weeks, and enjoyed my stay. After my two probationary weeks, I became a runner at Headquarters. My job was to take new arrivals through the same procedure that I had followed on my first day in camp.

We signed in—there were seven of us—and the simple camp rules were explained to us by Mr. Adams, an elderly man with white hair who held the title of Executive Officer. He wore blue jeans and a blue work shirt, and the top button of his shirt was buttoned, even though he didn't have a tie. Mr. Adams had once been a bank president, and, with the help of two clerks, he did all of the camp paperwork. The camp commandant, a big paunchy man in his early forties, had once been the chief of police in Wilkes-Barre, Pennsylvania. He commanded the camp by his physical presence. He never said a word to anyone, but at mealtimes he stood in the mess hall scowling, with his arms behind his back. He held a closed door meeting in his office every morning with his three captains, of A, B, and

77

C companies, and I suppose he passed out oral instructions to them. When he wasn't walking around the camp he stayed in the office with the door closed. He had his bunk in his office, too. I sat on a bench outside his office for three weeks, directly across from the railed enclosure where Mr. Adams and his two clerks worked, and the commandant never said a single word to me in all that time. The only people he addressed directly were Mr. Adams and the three captains, and he only talked with them in private.

If there was a disciplinary problem, the captain of the company concerned explained it to Mr. Adams. Mr. Adams then went into the commandant's office, obtained the decision, and then informed the captain, who took care of the matter. There was no appeal from the commandant's decisions, and he was the only man who could decide whether a man would be given a second chance or not. However, I never heard of him ever giving anyone a second chance. A complaint by Mr. Adams or by any captain was enough to get the offender bounced out of the camp regardless of the charge. The offender was never allowed to explain his side of the story, either. As a disciplinary system, it was incredibly efficient.

After we heard the rules (stay clean, and do as you are told or get out), we were marched over to the supply tent. We were each issued a towel and a bar of soap. We went then to the showers, took one, and were assigned to a camp cot in one of the probation tents. There were eight cots to a tent, with two army blankets per cot, and no pillow. We kept the tent clean and marched to meals where we ate at the same table, but we weren't given any work assignments until the two weeks had passed. I was then given a cot in the barracks, and assigned to Headquarters as a runner.

The hardest part of the runner's job, I learned when I

got it, was coaxing some of the bums into taking the mandatory shower. None could deny that he needed one. The water was fairly hot, or warm enough, but in December and January it was cold at night, especially when the eastbound freights came in. And many new arrivals, after walking out to the camp from the yards, simply didn't want to take a shower. At least one bum in ten refused, and I had to tell Mr. Adams. He, in turn, told the commandant. The man's unused towel and bar of soap were collected from him, and he was then escorted to the front gate by one of the CPs. I didn't care personally whether a man took a shower or not, but because Mr. Adams knew the percentage of those who would refuse to take one, I could only let one slip through once in awhile. If I had been caught letting a man get by without a shower, I would have been escorted to the gate myself, so the only way a bum could get out of it was to bribe me with a dime or a sack or two of Bull Durham. On the other hand, I never asked for a bribe.

There is a definite distinction, and an important one, to be made between a bum (tramp) and a hobo (transient worker). A bum, or tramp, is a professional; he is on the road by choice, and he is uninterested in employment of any kind. A hobo is a man who uses freight trains as a free means to get from one job to another, especially during harvest seasons. The hobo frequents the jungles and uses the trains just as bums do, and he is not above begging when he is broke, but he is on the road primarily in search of employment. In the American economy, bums and hobos are a constant.

But in the 1930s there was another in-between category, a man who was homeless and who would much rather have been settled somewhere, anywhere, with a permanent job of some kind. He was on the road because he had nowhere else to go, and he hated his condition. The latter, just as the Chicano had told me, had found a home in the Tucson transient camp, and many of these men were, indeed, sweating out the Depression in the camp. Mr. Adams was one of the new Depression breed of homeless men who had arrived in Tucson by freight train, although he was one of the most brilliant men I have ever met. It seemed absurd to me that a man of his capabilities worked so hard for only ninety cents a week, but then it had been equally absurd for the former symphony conductor I had worked with in Los Angeles to sell the *L.A. Examiner* on the street corner. At least Mr. Adams, in his position of Executive Officer, was entitled to a "Mr." and he probably needed this formality for his self-esteem.

These new transient camps, at Tucson, Yuma, Douglas (and, eventually, in Prescott), all worked out well, and it was a kind of miracle that they did and that the right bums were found to administer them. But then the right bums were not exactly bums, hobos, or road kids like me—they were misplaced bourgeois. Except for the Yuma camp, which according to rumor had a petty tyrant as the commandant, these were all highly successful camps, and the Arizonans had shown unusual wisdom by letting the inmates run their own camps without interference.

Several crates of books had been donated to the camp by the Tucson townspeople, and because I had nothing better to do during my probationary period, I read *Oliver Twist, Typee, Innocents Abroad,* and the tales of Edgar Allan Poe. Between meals of plentiful, if starchy, food, reading was a great way to kill time, and these were all enjoyable books to read.

I also practiced, until I could do it quickly and easily, rolling a cigarette with Bull Durham tobacco and brown wheatstraw papers, using only one hand. I had plenty of extra papers, and I sat cross-legged on my cot, with a spread newspaper to catch the loose flakes of tobacco, and practiced it until I had it down perfectly. This is no great achievement, but it is a trick greatly admired by those who witness it, particularly by my fellow soldiers when I later joined the regular Army. The trick is to roll a thin cigarette instead of a fat one, and to make certain there is a deeply hollowed space in the center of the little pile of tobacco in the paper before rolling it between forefinger, stiff middle fingers, and the thumb. The thumb nail should be at least a quarter-inch long beyond the tip, because the nail does most of the work. Anyone who has twelve or fifteen hours to spare can learn easily how to roll a cigarette with one hand. To conserve my tobacco, I usually rolled a cigarette about the same thickness as a kitchen match, which was only good for about four or five drags before it became too short to smoke. As a rule, I could have my tobacco and papers out, roll and smoke a cigarette and put my sack of tobacco away again before the average smoker could get his own cigarette rolled and lighted.

One day, on my way to the mess hall for lunch, I heard a man's voice shout from a tent I passed:

"Drop that knife, you cocksucker!"

The voice was absolutely chilling. I knew that there was a duel of some kind going on inside the tent, and that someone would soon be killed. It was all there, in the terror-stricken quality of the anguished voice. I stopped walking, wondering what to do. Whatever it was that was going on inside the tent was none of my business, and I certainly didn't want to get mixed up in a knife fight. But I entered the tent anyway, one of the bravest things I have ever done. What could I have done to stop the fight anyway? Certainly I couldn't have disarmed anyone with a knife.

But the only person in the tent was a one-armed man. He was about thirty, and he had lost his right arm a few inches above the elbow. The sewn stump was puckered, as though it had been pulled tight with a draw-string. The man was lying supine on his cot, and as soon as he saw the expression on my face he burst out with a jeering, raucous laugh. I was still looking around, wondering what had happened to the man with the knife.

"It works every time," the one-armed man said calmly, after he stopped laughing. "Have you got a smoke?"

"Only the makings," I said, taking out my tobacco and papers.

"That's okay," he said, lifting his stump to show it to me, "but I only got one arm. You'll have to roll it for me, but I'll do my own lickin'."

Without thinking about it, I rolled the cigarette with my right hand in about five seconds, and held it out to him so he could lick the paper.

"Stick it up your ass!" he said bitterly. Then he rolled over and faced the wall of the tent. I licked the paper myself, lit the cigarette, and left.

I was only about twenty yards away from the tent before he shouted again: *"Drop that knife, you cocksucker!"*

Even though I knew that he was all alone in the tent, the conviction and utter terror in his voice still sent shivers down my back. That one-armed man, I thought to myself, has lost touch with reality, but I have not—and that was a comfort.

There was a way to be sent home free from the camp. If a person had a home to go to, and if his story was checked out by Mr. Adams and by the American Red Cross in his home town, he was given a ticket, some eating money, and was put on the Sunset Limited, riding the cushions, for home.

Charles Ray Willeford II, and son. Little Rock, Arkansas, 1919.

Mattie Sawyers, the author's grandmother, with Charles. Little Rock, Arkansas, 1919.

The author with his parents in front of the First Mormon House,
Salt Lake City, Utah, 1920.

Aileen Willeford and Charles. Los Angeles, California, 1921.

Aileen and Charles. Los Angeles, California, 1922.

Charles, Aileen and Mattie. Long Beach, California, 1923.

Charles and Brownie. Los Angeles, California, 1923.

The author, a recruit on leave in Manila, Philippine Islands, 1937.

Although I didn't intend to go home (conditions had not changed there), I wanted to take advantage of this deal. The difficult part was in confessing my real name to Mr. Adams. I admired and respected him, and he had been very nice to me, and I thought that he would be disappointed in me when he found out that Jake Lowey was not my real name. But when I finally screwed up my courage to tell him the truth about myself, he just laughed.

"Okay, sonny boy," he said. "I'll see that you get home."

He wrote down the information, and sent a wire to the Red Cross in Los Angeles. Two days later, after the Red Cross had confirmed with my grandmother that I had a home to go to, I was taken to the Tucson RR station by a C.P. He took me into the chair car, handed my ticket to the conductor, and just a moment or so before the train left, handed me three silver dollars. The C.P. waited on the platform until the train left the station.

The Sunset Limited was a fast passenger train, and the journey from Tucson to Los Angeles was only an overnight trip. I got off the train at Yuma, however, about one-thirty A.M. I then walked up to the abandoned prison, and slept there for the rest of the night.

Taking stock the next morning, I decided that I was in fair economic shape. I had new work shoes, blue jeans, and a blue denim work shirt. I still had my roughneck sweater, baseball cap, and my blue-and-white necktie. I had gained a few pounds on the starchy camp diet, and my new short haircut would last for another six weeks or so before it needed cutting again. I had more than six dollars in cash because I had resisted the temptation to eat on the train in the expensive dining car. I had thrown away the other clothes I had started out with, and I had a deep desert tan. My split upper lip still hurt when I laughed or smiled, but I smiled rarely and I had developed a new habit of listening instead of talking. I also had a good supply of tobacco and cigarette papers.

If I expected to go to Chicago, my chosen destination, I had to head east again, through Tucson, and then on to Douglas and El Paso. My immediate problem was to get through Tucson without running into Mr. Adams or the camp police. But then, no one would actually be looking for me in the RR yards in Tucson, so I wasn't too concerned about getting through, except that it would be a long haul of 400 miles or more across the state from Yuma to Douglas before I could safely leave the train.

After leaving the prison that morning, I bought some candy bars and a quart of soda water in town. Then I walked beyond the town to the water tower where the bums were supposed to catch the train. There was very little yard activity at Yuma, and bums were not allowed to catch the freights east when they were still easy to board at a standstill. Instead, we had to wait outside town and catch the train while it was moving at about fifteen miles per hour. That isn't too fast if a man knows what he is doing, and I could latch onto a boxcar that was traveling twenty-five miles an hour. But when a train is going faster than twenty-five miles an hour, it is best to stand still and watch it go by. There will always be another day, another train.

About a mile past the water tower there was pile of creosoted telephone poles, and a road kid was sitting on top of them. He was about twelve or thirteen, rail-thin, with freckles and a pinched face. He told me a bitter story.

He had walked out to the new transient camp outside Yuma, a tent city on the site of an abandoned airfield, and the camp policeman on the main gate had refused to let him in. The camp no longer took in juveniles, the guard told the kid. At first the camp had taken in juveniles, runaways, and the like, but after two kids were punked by

84

older bums in the camp and had complained about it to the cops in Yuma, the camp commandant had decided that the best way to avoid such problems in the future was to ban juveniles from the camp. Of course, the kid had tried to lie to the guard about his age, but because he couldn't show any documentary proof he had been turned away.

He had then walked the four miles back to Yuma. He could have slept at the Yuma police station, he said, but then he would have, in all probability, been kept in the jail until his family was notified. He had no family to notify, he claimed, but they wouldn't have believed him. When they finally did find out that he had no family, he would have had to stay in jail until the welfare people in Yuma could find a foster home for him somewhere. That could have taken years, so he had said the hell with it, and he had decided to head on out of Yuma and go to Tucson.

"Did you eat yet?" I said, offering him a candy bar.

He shook his head, but refused the candy. "I got me some day-olds," he held up a sack, "from nickeling-up on a bakery."

Nickeling up meant going into a bakery with a nickel and a sad expression and asking for as much stale bread as could be spared for a nickel. Strangely enough, without a nickel you would get little or nothing. But with a nickel a baker would usually give you a loaf of bread and throw in a batch of stale donuts, cookies, and sweet rolls as well.

Altogether, this kid had walked about twelve miles with holes in both shoes, so he had blisters on his heels and on the soles of both feet. He looked exhausted.

"D'you think there'll be any empties?"

"No," I said, "not on the Pacific Fruit Express, although they sometimes put on an empty gondola. The last time I rode to Tucson, I had to ride on top of a reefer. So you'd better take some water."

"I don't have no water."

"Okay." I shrugged, resolving not to ride on the same car with the kid and share my bottle of soda water with him, although I would have given him a candy bar. "Maybe you can get some water when the train stops at Gila Bend."

When we heard the engine highball in the yards, we climbed down from the telephone poles and started walking up the well-defined gandy dancer's trail alongside the tracks. As the engine passed me, I started running. I managed to get up to train speed by the time the fourth boxcar came by, and I caught the ladder rungs at the front of the fifth boxcar. The train was moving a little faster than fifteen miles an hour, and I banged my left knee against the board walls of the car as I was swung against it by the momentum of the train. I looked back and saw that the kid, instead of catching the front end of the sixth car as a man is supposed to do, had tried for the back end of the same car I caught. And he had tried to grab onto the ladder with only one hand while carrying his bag of bakery stuff in the other. He had, of course, been snatched off the ground by the momentum, but there had been nothing to stop his swing; just empty space between the cars. As he lost his grip, he had been swung between the cars, and he fell. He must have pushed out some as he fell, and was on the ground with his head toward the back of the moving train, lying very still. I hesitated, but only for a second or so. I faced the engine and started running with my feet before I jumped off and hit the ground, but by this time the train was moving at about twenty-five miles an hour. When I hit, I tumbled and landed on my right shoulder. The bottle of soda water slipped out of my shirt and the neck broke off. I wasn't hurt very much, except for a few scratches on my right cheek from the loose gravel beside the tracks. A sharp stone was embedded in the heel of my palm, and I had twisted my foot slightly—just enough to feel a twinge.

As I walked back up the trail the crummy, or the caboose, passed me before I got back to where the kid was sprawled out on the ground. He wasn't moving, and his pinched face was as white as a peeled almond. One arm was across his eyes, as if he were shielding them from the sun, and his other arm was limp in the dirt. Blood gushed from his right knee, and I looked away from it. His right foot, with the shoe still on it, was in the center of the tracks, about ten yards away from where he was lying. I knew that I had to get some help for him quickly, but I wondered how to get it. If I went back to the Yuma RR station, would they believe me if I told them there was a kid hurt down the tracks? And if they believed me, would they care? How could I make them see the seriousness of the kid's injury? I knew immediately what I had to do, of course, but I still didn't want to do it. But time was passing, and I knew that if I didn't do something in a hurry the kid would bleed to death.

I picked up the severed foot, cradled it to my chest, and started running down the gandy dancer's trail beside the tracks. I kept a steady jog, a rate I knew I could maintain. When I reached the station I went inside and put the foot down on the ticket counter. Out of breath, or almost out of breath, and with a stitch in my side, I pointed down the tracks and told the man on the other side of the counter that a kid down there was hurt. A uniformed brakeman took my arm and led me over to one of the waiting room benches and told me to sit down. I sat down heavily, dizzily, put my head between my knees, and passed out cold— just like that.

That is how I lost my baseball cap. It must have fallen

off when I jumped from the moving boxcar and tumbled on the ground.

When I woke later, still on the bench, someone had put a pillow under my head and covered me with a blanket. I was still a little dizzy as I sat up, but I rolled a cigarette. I had to use both hands to roll it, and my fingers trembled as I lit it. A middle-aged man wearing a gray suit, a gray rancher's hat, and a gray silk tie with a hand-painted picture of a dog's head on it, sat beside me. His voice was solemn and gravelly.

"You okay?"

I nodded.

"Come with me."

I followed him into a small office in the station, and sat in the chair he pointed to, as he picked up some paper forms from the desk.

"Just sign these forms on the lines where I've marked a little red X," he said.

I signed the papers, "Jake Lowey," on the X-marked lines. The forms were printed in some kind of legalese language, but I didn't read them.

"Where're you headed, Jake?" the man asked.

"El Paso," I said. "My daddy owns a clothing store there. He sent me to L.A. to buy some pants at a warehouse sale, but I was held up by robbers on Alameda Street, and they took all my money. That's why I was trying to catch a freight—to get back home to El Paso."

"Don't overdo it, Jake. I'll see that you get to El Paso. Stay here."

I waited in the cluttered little office. Later, tne man in gray brought me an XLNT hot tamale and an enameled metal cup of coffee. The tamale was barely warm, and I ate it out of the corn husk wrapper. When the eastbound Sunset Limited came through, the man in gray took me out to the chair car, told me to sit down, and called the conductor down to the seat.

"See that this young man," he told the conductor, "gets safely to El Paso, and see to it that he doesn't get off the train until he does."

"Yes, sir," the conductor said.

I never found out what happened to the kid who lost his foot, and I have never really wanted to know. I suspect the worst, but as long as I don't know I can still hope that he survived. The man in the gray suit was, in all probability, a railroad bull, but from the quiet authority he seemed to have, for all I know, he might have been the president of the railroad. No ticket was issued for my trip, and the conductor, an elderly white-haired man, kept a nervous eye on me most of the way to El Paso. When the train paused for its ten-minute stop in Tucson, I stayed prudently in the men's room, and I didn't look out the window.

6

The Depression, it seemed to me, had hit El Paso worse than it had Los Angeles. Perhaps this first impression was caused by the lack of greenery and by the yellow dust that had settled over everything. The drought that had settled over the plains states had also reached southwest Texas. In Los Angeles, there were still areas of affluence, but not in El Paso. There also seemed to be a higher percentage of ragged Mexicans in El Paso, and they weren't confined to certain areas of town, like they were in L.A. The railroad yards, and the surrounding neighborhoods, are the most unattractive sections of any city, but even downtown El Paso had a grim and grimy face. Even if the Mexicans weren't counted, the transient population was enormous, with shabby men wandering about the mean streets in an effort to ding marks almost as badly off as themselves. To bum a back door handout it was necessary to walk to residential areas a good many blocks from the yards and downtown. There was no chance of getting a handout within six or seven blocks of the yards. Those poor residents had been hit too many times. They had, as a consequence, from sheer necessity, steeled their minds against giving anybody anything again.

In the jungle, I ran into a group of four bums who had joined forces, pooling their sparse pickings to make a mulligan. One man had obtained a pound of rice, another a half-dozen turnips, another had some small new potatoes and a few onions, and another man (the cook) had two ragged heads of cabbage peppered with rotten black spots. They were boiling this mixture in a five gallon Standard gas can, and the cook was complaining about its lack of taste. I volunteered, in return for a portion of the mulligan, to go get some salt and pepper.

My offer was accepted, but my attempts to beg some salt and pepper were fruitless. Not only was I turned down at the houses I tried, I was treated to hard luck stories, and I was unable to get a small matchbox full of salt, which was all I needed. Of course, these were all houses near the yards, and they had the down-pointing arrows scratched on them with chalk or a nail by other bums who had learned that the residents were non-givers. But I didn't think that a man would be refused a little salt or perhaps a small newspaper twist of pepper. In the end, I bought a five-cent package of salt at a Mexican grocery store, and a handful of dried hot red peppers. Without salt, and without the addition of the crushed red peppers, the mulligan wouldn't have had any savor at all, so I was given a full portion of the stew for my contribution. After the cook salted the mulligan, I divided the remaining salt evenly with the others, and kept a matchboxful for myself.

The day before, according to my dinner companions, the police, or the "town clowns," as they were called, had descended on the jungle and decimated it. Decimation, apparently, was a practice that was followed throughout Texas at the time, and it was used by the law as a way to sell cheap labor to farmers at a small rake-off for the cops. After the sheriff and his deputies rounded up a bunch of bums in the jungle, they were placed in a straight line and then every tenth man was tapped on the shoulder from behind. The tapped men took one step forward, and were then loaded onto trucks and taken to farms to chop weeds or to pick vegetables under the direction of a few guards armed with shotguns. When the job was completed, whatever it happened to be, the bums were released; but they were not paid for their work—except for the meals they received from the farmer concerned. The danger of being decimated was present in every Texas jungle, but at least, as one bum put it, the process was fair and democratic, and in keeping with The American Way of Life. Every tenth man was tapped fairly, regardless of his physical condition, or whether he was young or old. No effort was made to pick out the strongest and fittest for the manual labor. Therefore, a lucky and healthy man could go undecimated forever, whereas some poor unlucky rummy and physical derelict might be tapped every time. These four men who told me about the practice were all fatalists, and they intended to stay in the jungle overnight by their fire. But not wishing to try my luck, I left the jungle, after filling up on the mulligan, and spent the night in a ten-cent flophouse bed downtown.

I stayed in El Paso for five days, wandering about the city and spending my money on cheap food and lodging. In any Mexican café, I could get a large bowl of chile con carne and a plateful of warm tortillas for a dime, and there was a small restaurant near the yards, just a notch or two in quality above the jungle beaneries, where I could buy six donuts and a cup of coffee for only six cents.

The flophouse, even at ten cents a night, was no bargain. In addition to the big welts I had on my body from bed-bugs, I picked up a family of crabs from the john. I borrowed a razor from the desk man at the flophouse, and shaved off my sparse pubic hair, and he gave me some kerosene to rub into the skin to kill the eggs. But some of the bedbug bites became infected from my scratching them. By an effort of will, I quit scratching altogether, and the bites eventually healed.

The reason I stayed in the flophouse to begin with was because it was too cold and windy to sleep outside. But then I discovered an abandoned shed behind a billboard in a vacant lot. The shed had once been a storehouse for tools of some kind, though there was nothing in the old shed now except a small work-bench and the nails on the walls where the tools had been hung. I slept there at night instead of going to the flophouse, and it was a snug place to be when the wind howled outside. In the mornings I went down to the breadline at the yards for a breakfast of vegetable stew, a piece of bread, and either coffee or cocoa. Even the breadline, however, was not immune from being decimated from time to time, although I was never caught in any of the round-ups.

According to all reports, it was still snowing farther

north in New Mexico, from Tucumcari on, so I had no desire to travel on into that cold weather toward an even colder Chicago. At the same time, I didn't believe that I could survive for the rest of the winter in El Paso. My money was dribbling away, as tight as I was with it, and when it was gone I knew there would be no way to get any more in a city as depressed as El Paso. Nor did I relish the possibility of getting decimated and spending one or two weeks chopping weeds with a short-handled hoe down in Fabens, Texas.

Like the other bums on the road, I paid no attention to Christmas, which was, in road parlance, "just another day to ride the train," nor did I pay much attention to my fourteenth birthday. I was fourteen, but I didn't feel any differently, although I did think that a new January and a new year should be a better one than the year that had passed. As I wandered aimlessly about the chilly, dusty, and windy El Paso streets I regretted the impulse that had led to my leaving the camp in Tucson. The three dollars I had earned by leaving had not been worth it, because I could have spent a very pleasant winter in the Tucson camp. I couldn't go back, of course, not after defrauding the state by taking the ticket and the per diem money to go home, but I could, I decided, check into the new transient camp at Douglas, Arizona, under a new name. No one would be the wiser, or know that I had been given transportation home from Tucson. Even if I were recognized by another bum, he would be unlikely to say anything. The time to leave El Paso was now, while I still had a little cash, and not wait until I had spent everything in this depressing city.

The next morning, after nickeling up at a bakery, I caught an empty for Douglas, Arizona. I didn't know how crowded the new camp would be, and I wanted to make certain I

93

could get in, so I didn't tell any of the bums in my boxcar about the camp. My blue work shirt and pants, however, were standard camp issue, and would be a dead giveaway, so I traded the new pants for a patched pair of well-worn bib overalls with a man in the boxcar. The overalls, worn over my shirt and necktie, would serve me well as a disguise until my two weeks of probation were over with and I could get new clothes from the Douglas camp.

Agua Prieta, the small town in Old Mexico across the border from Douglas, Arizona, was better known in America than Douglas. Agua Prieta had been the Mexican town where Aimee Semple McPherson, the evangelist, had turned up in the mid-twenties with her wild story about being kidnapped and held prisoner in the desert. She had escaped, she claimed, and walked across miles of desert until she reached Agua Prieta. Her long red hair was freshly washed, and she was unsunburned and beautifully made-up, and, as it turned out later on, she had been shacking up with her lover in the vicinity of San Diego. But Aimee wasn't hurt too badly by the scandal. Aimee's Angelus Temple, in L.A., was greatly admired by many people in southern California because Aimee gave away food and clothing to the poor. I remembered the name, Agua Prieta, from hearing the scandal discussed by my grandmother and her friend, Marie Weller, but I didn't go into the Mexican town until I had finished my two probationary weeks at the Douglas camp and was entitled to a Saturday night pass.

Except for the drafty old airplane hangar that served as a messhall and kitchen, the Douglas camp was a tent city. There was also a long narrow building, formerly a ranch-house, that served as a headquarters, supply room, and infirmary (there were four double-bunk beds). The showers and latrines were open to the sky, although they were enclosed by canvas flys. Pyramidal army tents held eight men apiece, and again, like the camp in Tucson, there were three companies, A, B, and C. The Douglas commandant, however, had divided the three companies roughly into age groups: young, middle-aged, and elderly. This was a good idea, I thought. The old bums had given up for the most part, and they were secretive and crochety. They liked to lie on their bunks and doze quietly between meals. The middle-aged men bragged about their successes in the recent past, or tried to make things out of toothbrush handles they could peddle in town. The younger men were boisterous, and they liked to play grabass and tell lies. Company B, the more or less middle-aged company, was a settling or stabilizing factor, because the men in B Company had a tendency to stay put. The old bums in Company C, who were used to independence, moved out within a very few days, unless they were sick, and there was a fast turnover among the younger men as well.

I lucked into a good job. A Chicano in my tent, Pablito Figueras, who came from Whittier, California (he had spent three years in the reformatory there for youthful offenders), was a barber. Pablito, together with two other, older barbers, had set up a shop in one corner of the hangar messhall, about twenty yards from the dining area. Pablito got me the job as their clean-up man. I swept and mopped the barber shop floor, and ran errands for the three barbers. After my two weeks probation, I got my ninety cents a week from the camp payroll, and each barber gave me thirty cents a week. The barbers charged ten cents for a haircut and ten cents for a shave, and, in comparison with the rest of the camp personnel, they were affluent men. And now that I was dragging in $1.80 a week, I felt on top of things myself. After all, I thought, I'm earning twice as much money each week as the camp commandant. But this wasn't true, because of the small exchange store in camp that was run by the commandant's punk. The small store sold candy bars, soda pop, snuff and tobacco, needles and thread, and razor blades. The commandant, of course, got his rake-off from the store.

The commandant was a scary-looking, bear-like man, with a shaved head and a scarred and slightly disfigured face. He had two dishonorable discharges, one from the U.S. Army and one from the Marines, in black frames on the office wall behind his desk. Even the camp police, who were chosen for their height and bulk, not for their brains, were afraid of the commandant. Every morning at ten, the commandant came to the barber shop for a free skull and face shave from Pablito Figueras. It was ostensibly free, that is. When the commandant got up from the home-made barber chair, which was made from unpainted two-by-fours, he always said to Pablito:

"Chalk it up, Figueras, and give yourself a nickel tip."

"Gracias, Commandante, gracias!" Playing servile Mexican, Pablito would grin widely and bob his head, and chalk up the job to experience.

Oddly enough, the other two barbers, both of them middle-aged, were jealous of Pablito because the commandant never gave them the opportunity to shave the misshapen skull and ugly scarred face.

On my first Saturday night pass, I went into Agua Prieta with Pablito. He was a drinker, uninterested in women, and every Saturday night he drank himself into unconsciousness in the same cantina. Naturally enough, the cantina proprietor always greeted him warmly, and when he passed out the proprietor let him sleep at the table for the rest of the night. He would then wake him at dawn. Broke, or nearly so, Pablito would walk back to camp, and then earn enough money during the week for another big drunk the next Saturday night. But I wasn't interested in getting drunk. I wanted to get laid. In Company A, among the younger men, getting laid was the main topic of conversation, and I was eager to have this experience for the first time.

Pablito bought me a bottle of beer, my first, which I was unable to finish. I couldn't abide the bitter taste. After eating a few tacos with him, I left the cantina and walked to the far edge of town to the house of blue lights. This was purported to be the best whorehouse in Agua Prieta. There were several girls in the bar area, and they formed a rough line when I came in to look them over. When I hesitated, unable to make a decision, one of them selected me by grabbing my hand. She was a young woman, mocha-colored, with wide soft hips, a white blouse, and a long red skirt. We went outside and around to the other side of the building where each girl had a separate room with a private door to the dirt street. She closed the door and took off her skirt and blouse. She then knelt in front of a garishly colored magazine illustration of Jesus Christ on the cross. The picture was lighted from below by a candle in a blue glass. She crossed herself, rose, came over to where I was standing, and checked my cock for V.D. I didn't get an erection. She then washed my cock with a dishcloth, using a sliver of soap and a shallow panful of tepid water. I still didn't respond, and knew that I would not, regardless of what she tried to do to me. I gave her thirty cents, the going rate, buttoned up, and opened the door to the street.

"No teep?" she said.

"No." I shook my head. "No tip."

The woman hadn't been surprised, nor did she make any effort to keep me in the room. She assumed, I supposed, that I had already been with a girl earlier in the evening. But I had not, of course. Her kneeling posture in front of the religious picture, and then crossing herself before grabbing my cock had sent chills down my back. Although I was not a religious person, there was no way that I could commit fornication in the same room with a shrine. My chances of finding a Protestant woman in Agua Prieta were negligible, so I knew I must wait to commit the big sin with some indifferent Jewish or Protestant woman back in the States. I was not a Catholic, so I was not concerned with the state of my so-called soul, but I was concerned deeply with the state of that Catholic whore's soul. I could not, knowingly, contribute to her execution of a mortal sin.

When I returned to the cantina, Pablito was already drunk, having switched over from beer to mescal. I tried to talk to him, but he was on the near-verge of incoherence. I left him there, and walked the four-and-a-half miles back to camp. Except for the marquee lights of the movie theater, the main street of Douglas was unlighted, and there were no people in evidence. The main business in town was a smelter that melted the copper ore that was mined in Bisbee, a few miles away, but otherwise, the little city was like a ghost town. There was nothing to do at night, so they all went to bed early.

7
_____

Two uneventful weeks later, two men wearing dark business suits and gray fedoras arrived in camp in a black Ford phaeton. They left with the commandant, and he was never heard from again. There were all kinds of rumors about this event, but no one knew for certain who the two men were, or what they had wanted with him. He was hand-cuffed with both hands behind his back, according to one witness, but another man claimed that he was merely hand-cuffed to the wrist of one of the men who came for him. Some said that the commandant was wanted for murder, which was easy enough to believe, and others said that he was an escaped convict, but no one knew for sure. With little else to do except talk, there was a good deal of speculation. It had happened and he was gone, but at least there was something new to talk about for a few days. The executive officer, Mr. Sealy, was now in charge of the camp, but we heard that he would soon be replaced by a new commandant, and that there was no chance that Mr. Sealy, who was only five-two, would get the job. On an errand to the supply room to pick up some towels for the barbers, I entered the office and took a look at the two framed dishonorable discharges that were still on the wall behind the commandant's desk. The dishonorable discharge from the Marines, I noticed, was either printed on yellow paper, or had faded to yellow, but I couldn't tell for sure. I talked to Pablito about it, and he said that the Marines had printed their dishonorable discharges on yellow parchment, but the practice was now discontinued. At any rate, the ex-commandant had been proud of his discharges, so I knew he wouldn't have willingly left them behind.

Three days later, Mr. Adams arrived. He came down to Douglas on the Sunset Limited from Tucson to be our new commandant. I was sweeping the floor in the barber shop when he entered the hangar, accompanied by a camp guard. He had just taken over, and was making his initial inspection of the camp. He spotted me almost at once, and pointed to me. Raising his voice, he said to the guard:

"Kick that bastard's ass all the way to the gate!"

With the C.P. right behind me I started running, so he only managed to kick me once, a glancing blow on the outer part of my left leg, before I reached the gate. The gate was open, with another C.P. stationed there. As I whipped by him in a cloud of dust, he just laughed, and made no effort to detain me. I pounded down the road toward town, but when I saw that I wasn't being chased I quit running, and walked the rest of the way without looking back.

I was on my own again, which I didn't mind particularly, but seeing Mr. Adams again had filled me with remorse. If I had known that he was coming as the new commandant I would have left before he arrived. I had failed and disappointed him, and he had a right to be angry. He had probably heard from my grandmother, either directly or from the Red Cross, when I had failed to arrive in Los Angeles. So he knew that I had reneged, or, if he hadn't heard from Mattie, just seeing me in the camp was proof enough that I hadn't gone home.

I had my money on me, happily, but not my sweater. My sweater, the old pair of bib overalls, and the little cloth bag of toilet articles that had been issued to everyone by the Red Cross, and six sacks of Bull Durham were back in my tent. But the clothes I was wearing were new, I had my necktie, and I also had my money. I was still much better off than the day I had signed into the Douglas camp. My big regret was leaving Pablito: I had been pressuring him to teach me how to cut hair, and he had said that he would. This was something I had wanted to learn. With a comb and a pair of scissors, a barber—even a drunk like Pablito—can go anywhere in the world and always make a living, or at least pick up some money to eat on. Here was another lost opportunity.

A local freight left Douglas each night for Rodeo, New Mexico, and there was the regular Pacific Fruit Express that by-passed Rodeo and went directly to El Paso via Lordsburg, New Mexico. The trains were about three hours apart, and I could catch either one of them. But they wouldn't leave until late that night. I had a long day to kill.

I crossed the border into Agua Prieta, and went to Pablito's favorite cantina and ordered a dozen tacos. The cantina was cool and dark, and the padded chair with its back to the adobe wall was comfortable. Tacos, all tightly rolled, sold for a dime a dozen. They were rolled like large cigars, and they were very hot. I rejected a beer, but nodded when the waiter suggested a mescalito. Pablito always drank mescal, and he told me that it was ten times better than tequila.

Mescal, like tequila, is made from cactus, and the clear liquid has little white flecks in it that resemble bits of sperm. But these white particles are merely tiny bits of cactus pulp. You can also tell a bottle of mescal from a bottle of tequila because mescal, to be authentic, has a preserved earthworm (*gusano*) in each bottle. I took a small sip, to test it, and entered into a dubious friendship with mescal. The small sip was a warm and loving ball that entered my throat, rolled gently down to my stomach like an unexpected gift, and then diffused like searching white-hot tendrils into every part of my body. There was a faint but not unpleasant aftertaste of gasoline—one of my favorite odors—and when I bit into another taco, it now seemed so mild I had to add a teaspoon of hot salsa to bring back the flavor. But neither the delicious tacos nor the two mescalitos that followed were enough to break the sodden gloom that overwhelmed me. My body tingled with well-being, and I was as sensitive to color and light as a chameleon, but my mental state was as dark as the black creek that gave the tiny Mexican town its name.

Depression, I found out several years later, is a state common to mescal drinkers, but most drinkers are willing to suffer it gladly because the accompanying physical feeling of well-being practically eliminates hunger and bodily pain.

By the time I finished my second mescalito I was no longer hungry, and I left the remaining tacos on the plate. With mescal, I didn't need anything else. All I could think about was what an awful person I had become. I had let Mr. Adams down, a man I admired and respected, but worse, much worse, I had done irreparable harm to Mattie, my poor grandmother, the only person in the world who had ever loved me. God knows she must have worried about me when I didn't come home on the day I had left Los Angeles. But then, when she was told by the Red Cross that I was on my way home from Tucson and I still hadn't come home, what additional suffering had I caused the poor woman? She must have suspected foul play, or a terrible accident, or even a kidnapping—who knows? And as the days passed, day after day, without a word from me, what did she think of me? How could I possibly do something so thoughtless and cruel to this poor old lady? Here I was, out on the road, enjoying myself, and I hadn't even written Mattie a letter to tell her how well I was doing out on my own. These thoughts, and more dismal thoughts like them, soon had me in tears.

In a novel, a brooding place like this is called a "plateau." In every third or fourth chapter, the protagonist has to run through a mental summary of some kind to keep the woolgathering reader informed about what has gone on already, and what will probably come to pass. This plateau is necessary so the reader won't forget some important point

that he has already read, but doesn't remember too well—
or remember at all.

But this book is not a novel. My remorse was real, and
I detested the person I had become. I thought of all the
good things my grandmother had done for me, and all of
the terrible things I had done in return. By my fourth
mescalito, however, at a nickel a shot, my deep, self-en-
gendered depression had escalated to deep apathy. Then,
when the plump middle-aged whore sat beside me, and
brushed the tears away from my cheeks with a soft hand,
and asked me if I wanted to go upstairs, I got a hard-on.

This woman also had a religious picture on the wall. But
she didn't kneel in front of it, nor did she cross herself
before she took me into her bed, a creaky springless bed
with a mattress stuffed with corn husks. Because of the
mescal, an inhibiting factor, I was able to last for almost
twenty minutes (some kind of record for a male virgin),
and then I went downstairs for more mescal.

The afternoon passed in a beautiful golden reverie, with
my physical well-being enhanced, not diminished, by the
professional piece of ass. Because I had already reached
the nadir of my depression before going upstairs, my
thoughts, by the time it got dark, were concerned with
how much better I would treat my aunt when I got to
Chicago, and how exciting and full my life would be when
I got my job on the midway at the Chicago World's Fair.

Then, with yet another mescalito, my mind sharpened,
and I began to think with a keen clarity. I realized, with a
frightful insight, that I did not have an aunt in Chicago, or
anywhere else. I had never been to Chicago. Nor did I
have any barker's job waiting for me on the midway at the
Fair. As I gradually got drunker, the fantasy of my made-
up cover story had fused with my real situation in my effort
to escape from my dark depression. I lurched up and away

from the table, and bought an eight-ounce bottle of mescal from the bartender. He poured the mescal from his bar bottle into a used catsup bottle, and then put a cork in it. At twenty-five cents an eight-ounce bottle, it was much cheaper than it was to keep buying one-ounce shots at a nickel a glass.

Three or four small raggedy boys attached themselves to me as I walked unsteadily toward the house of blue lights on the far edge of town. They begged me for pennies, but I cursed them and told them to get the hell away from me. They just laughed and followed me anyway, so I tried to ignore them. When I paused to have a pull from my bottle, they giggled with delight and shouted, "*Borracho!*" But I was a long way from being drunk, at least in my mind, even though my legs were rubbery. My mind was clear, and I wanted another girl, a younger girl than the middle-aged whore at the cantina.

I entered the bar at the house of blue lights and sat at a table by the hardpacked adobe dance floor. I put my bottle inside my shirt and ordered a mescalito from the waiter. Three girls sat at the table next to mine and jabbered at me in Spanish. I was supposed to choose one of them and invite her to my table. If I wouldn't do that, they wanted me to buy all of them a *cerveza*. I only knew a few words of Spanish—just those I had picked up on the playground at John Adams Junior High—but I could understand what they wanted all right. On the other side of the dance floor, a man started to play a guitar and sing, and his voice was so beautiful and the song was so sad that I began to cry. When he finished the song, I tossed him a quarter and he sang another. Weeping, I drank my fresh drink and ordered another, but before I finished the new one nausea gripped me. I barely made it outdoors before my insides erupted. One of the whores held my forehead in the palm of her hand as I leaned over the hitching rail outside the cantina. When I was breathing normally again she left me and went back inside. I was breathing much easier now. I crossed the patio and sat on a stone bench beside the well. The blue lights that encircled the roof of the cantina made little circles in the air. When I closed my eyes the bench whirled. When I opened them the bench stopped whirling. I had a long pull from my bottle and closed my eyes again. I left the bench and circled upward in a gradually narrowing spiral flight, ascending into the starry sky. The stars, blue and white, made little orbits of their own in the dark sky, and it was a beautiful sight. There was a tugging at my feet, as if the earth was unwilling to release me. I kicked out and I was alone and floating in the blackness of an endless night, and far beyond the stars.

I awoke shivering.

My teeth were chattering with cold, and a stiff gelid wind battered my naked body. Except for my blue-and-white necktie, which had a small knot tied so tight it couldn't be undone (I could only slip the tie over my head without untying it), I didn't have a stitch of clothes left. The tugging at my feet I had felt, just before I had passed out, had undoubtedly been those Mexican boys pulling off my new work shoes. I had been well out of everything when they had stripped off the rest of my clothes. They had even taken my bottle of mescal, although there couldn't have been much liquor left in it. The night was very dark, and there were no lights anywhere. The cantina was closed and shuttered, and they had switched off the little blue lights. But the lights at the border station, I knew, were very bright. Not only were the Mexican and the U.S. border offices well-lighted, there was a very bright overhead streetlight that illuminated the twenty-five yard stretch between the two customs offices. If I arrived naked at the

Mexican office, I would be arrested, and, if the Mexicans didn't arrest me, the U.S. border patrolman would put me in jail. The border patrolman would simply call for the Douglas police.

I gagged a little as I sat up, but there was nothing left inside me to throw up. My forehead hurt, and there was a sharp throbbing pain behind my eyes. Shivering like a dog passing broken glass, I got shakily to my feet and tried to get my bearings. I was southwest of town, with only a very few widely spaced adobe houses between me and the dirt road into the Mexican interior and the Sonoran desert. If I walked beyond these remaining houses, and then made a wide circle to my right, into the desert, I could cross the creek about two miles away from the border checkpoints and be back in Arizona without going through the official gateways.

Still shivering uncontrollably, I walked into the wind, head down, crept by the sleeping adobe houses and barking pariah dogs, and made a wide looping circle into the desert. I worried about stepping on a sharp rock, or perhaps on a sleeping rattler, with my bare feet. But I kept moving and the cold wasn't so devastating now that my blood was circulating. It was frightening, however, when bulky unexpected tumbleweeds, driven by the strong wind, came out of nowhere and bounced lightly off my naked body. I was able to keep my bearings without any trouble because, when I reached the shallow creek, I could see the lights from the two border stations and the bright streetlight between them. The water in the creek came barely to my ankles. On the other side, back in Arizona, I focused on the distant light that came from the all night smelter, which was hard by the railroad yards. I headed for the light, watching the ground for hazards, and then looking up again at the distant light as I threaded my way across the desert.

I was able to dodge the scattered clumps of chapparal and cacti because they were darker shapes against the black and distant mountains behind Douglas. Eventually, and with very sore feet, I reached the spur tracks of a siding. I then walked the ties of the spur into the yards. Before I reached the jungle, southeast of the yards, I picked up a piece of newspaper and held it in front of me, waist high, trying to block some of the wind. There was a single fire burning in the jungle, with two silhouetted figures sitting on the ground across from one another. I stopped about fifty yards away from the fire and called out:

"Hey, 'Bo!'"

"Hey, 'Bo!'" a black man's voice called back. "Who dat callen 'Hey, 'Bo'?"

"Me," I said, and I walked up to the fire so they could see me.

That's how I met Pearson and Billy Tyson.

Pearson, after he finished laughing, which took some time, removed his Chesterfield and put it around my shoulders. He then divested himself of some of his multi-layered clothing. He gave me a red-and-blue plaid flannel shirt (the third shirt under), and a pair of shabby tweed pants that were frayed slightly at the knees and cuffs. The tweed trousers were between his outer Big Boy work pants and his black wool suit pants. I slipped into the tweed pants and flannel shirt, and gave Pearson his overcoat back. The tweed pants, worn without underwear, were sticky and scratchy. Little twigs woven in the cloth worked their way out of the material occasionally and pricked my legs and backside, but they were warm. I was still barefooted, and I sat on the ground with my feet to the little fire, flexing my blue toes.

I had to tell and retell my story several times before Pearson and Billy Tyson were satisfied. Pearson was astonished by the easy way I had crossed the border back into Arizona. He had thought, or had been told, that there was an electrified barbed-wire fence along the entire length of the border between the U.S.A. and Old Mexico, and he was indignant and slightly alarmed about the idea that the U.S.A. was wide open to Mexicans; that hordes of Mexicans, if they had a mind to, could swarm into our country at will.

"What're your plans now, Jake?" Billy Tyson said.

"Well," I said, after thinking about it for a moment, "somehow or other, I've got to get a pair of shoes."

He nodded. "I'll tell you what, Jake. I'll help you get some shoes if you'll help me get a cowboy hat."

Billy Tyson, I soon discovered, was desperately homesick for his home back in Harlan County, Kentucky, but he couldn't go back until he got a cowboy hat. Before he left he had told all of his friends that he was going out West to become a cowboy. He had not, of course, become a cowboy, but he had gradually, piece by piece, acquired a cowboy costume. He had a pair of scuffed cowboy boots that were cripplingly tight in the toes, a pair of blue jeans, a denim jacket, and a scruffy sheepskin vest. He had obtained these clothes by trading with other bums, from the Goodwill department store in Dallas, and by theft. He also had a pair of worn leather gloves that were nicked and scarred from barbed wire. But until he could obtain a cowboy hat to complete his outfit, there was no way that he could return home and claim that he had been a cowboy. He didn't mind lying, or claiming that he had been a cowboy when he had not been one, but without the complete outfit—and the cowboy hat, next to the boots, was the most important item—his friends back in Harlan would never believe his story.

108

"Sure," I said. "I'll help you. It shouldn't be too hard to rustle up a cowboy hat."

But I was wrong; it was very difficult to obtain a cowboy hat. Billy Tyson didn't want a cheap straw cowboy hat. He wanted an authentic hat, a felt cowboy hat, and preferably a Stetson, the best cowboy hat ever made. The color was not of great importance to him, although his preference was for black, nor did the hat have to be brand new. A good Stetson cowboy hat lasted almost forever, anyway, so a used hat would be okay. A cowboy hat was a work hat, and it would hold water for a horse, if a cowboy's horse wanted a drink. But these ideal Stetson cowboy hats were so expensive that the cowboys who owned them—and there weren't that many cowboys left—rarely removed them from their heads. As a consequence, a cowboy hat was almost impossible to steal. Billy Tyson had been trying to find or steal a cowboy hat from Texarkana to El Paso, and from El Paso to Phoenix, and now back to Douglas, and so far he hadn't even come close to getting himself one. His boots were already too tight, and if he kept on growing, he might even have to get himself another pair of cowboy boots before he got his hat. But the one fact remained: Until he got his cowboy hat he could not go back home.

Billy Tyson had a mission in life—a goal. I was impressed.

"When you go to the back door and ask for a handout," I said, "d'you ever ask the woman if she's got a spare cowboy hat in the house? It seems to me that you might run into the widow of a cowboy, and she'll still have his hat to give you—"

Billy Tyson laughed derisively. "Cowboys don't get married, Jake. Didn't you know that? And if they ever did get hitched, and then died later on, they'd get buried with their hats. I seen it in movies. When they bury a cowboy on the lone prairie, they put his hat on his chest and fold his arms across it. It stays with him in the pine box."

"You're right," I agreed with him. "And in movies, anyway, that's the only time the other cowboys ever take off their hats, while the words are being said over the dead cowboy. They put their hats over their hearts, and then put 'em on again as soon as the trail boss finishes his little talk."

"That's right," Billy Tyson said. "You can't tell me nothen about cowboy hats I don't know already."

Pearson soon rolled himself into a black ball and went to sleep. Billy Tyson and I, taking turns gathering firewood, sat and talked by the fire for the rest of the night. It took me about a half-hour before I could fully understand his funny way of talking, but then I could understand him perfectly.

Pearson and Billy Tyson had been picked up in Phoenix by a cattle truck, and had ridden in the back, dodging two bellowing, pregnant cows, all the way to Bisbee. In Bisbee they had waited on the highway for about three hours, and then a man driving a Model A Ford had picked them up. He only drove about fifty yards before he stopped the car, and then he made them both ride in the rumble seat. They had almost froze back there before he let them off in Douglas. But they had smelled so bad from the cattle, the man couldn't have them sitting up front, he said.

They then decided to ride the freight train from Douglas to El Paso, but they had missed the last train by an hour by the time they got to the yards. They had baked some potatoes in the fire, and they were waiting, now, for the next freight out to El Paso.

Billy then told me about some of his adventures crossing Texas, including a long story about how he had evaded the notorious railroad bull, Texas Slim, in Longview, Texas. I had heard the identical story about dodging Texas Slim before, from a bum in the Tucson camp. And Billy had also heard it from someone before, too, I supposed, and then appropriated the story as his own. But the reinvention of or the appropriation of another man's story is common on the road, especially if the teller can show how deviously he has outwitted some town clown or railroad bull. So I didn't call Billy on it.

In turn, I told Billy Tyson about my aunt in Chicago, and about my promised job as a barker on the midway at the World's Fair. Both of us, who were fourteen, although I doubt that Billy was fourteen, as yet, told each other our true ages. And then we assured each other solemnly that we could both pass for seventeen. When a man has been alone and naked and suffering with a hangover in the desert, it is wonderful to encounter a sympathetic listener, so we became life-long friends.

In the morning, while Pearson remained in the jungle, Billy Tyson and I set off in opposite directions in Douglas in search of breakfast and shoes. There wasn't much point in Pearson's even trying to get anything to eat in Douglas. One of the bad features about having the new transient camps was that all of the Arizona residents knew about them now. As soon as a bum appeared at the back door and knocked, he was told by the resident about the camp, how to get there, and that he could eat and get free clothing there.

But I had a good excuse for begging in town. I was barefooted and my feet hurt, and I could display my stone bruises to prove it. I didn't feel that I could walk that far out to camp without any shoes, and besides, I said, I hadn't eaten for two days and I was faint with hunger. At the fourth house I tried, a big house with a tricycle in the yard, I lucked into a pair of black-and-white golf shoes, the kind with a fringed flap over the laces. The woman who gave me the shoes said that her husband had given up golf for the duration of the Depression, and that he had only worn them a few times. She also gave me a pair of wool pimento-and-black diamond knee socks to go with them, the kind that are worn with plus-fours. She gave me a cheese sandwich, a glass of milk and an orange, too. I saved the orange, and took it back to the jungle for Pearson's breakfast.

On the way back to the jungle, I stopped at a gas station and borrowed a pair of pliers. It took some time to unscrew all of the metal cleats from the golf shoes. The metal-ringed screwholes were still in the shoes, which made the soles clatter some on the asphalt streets as if I were wearing taps. The Argyle socks were thick and warm, however, and they helped to take up some of the slack in the shoes that were at least two-and-a-half sizes too large for me. I couldn't lift my feet off the ground much as I walked, or I would step right out of the shoes.

Billy Tyson got back to the jungle around noon, bringing a pair of ten-inch high rubber boots, full of holes, that he had found in an alley. He also brought a pork chop sandwich and an apple for Pearson. I threw the rubber boots away, but it would have been good to have them if I hadn't lucked into getting the golf shoes.

For the rest of the day we either slept or dozed under the pepper trees in the jungle. I then left and got a can full of water for the trip. That night we all caught the Pacific Freight Express to El Paso, riding in an empty boxcar crowded with ten more bums.

8

In El Paso, the three of us developed a sort of routine. In the mornings, early, after a breakfast of free vegetable stew at the yards breadline, we separated and foraged in the city for the rest of the day.

When a man doesn't know when or where his next meal is coming from, as soon as he finishes one meal, it is necessary to start looking for the next one. This incessant activity can result in both feast and famine, and a man soon becomes depressed either way by the stupidity of both options. I have been in the unhappy position of having to eat three different meals within an hour, forcing the last two down with great effort, having hit it too lucky and too soon between meals. I have also been unlucky, and I have gone as long as two days without eating anything at all. But that is the way it is; to survive on the road, a man cannot coast too long between meals. Given the limited options, it is better to be too full than it is to be too empty.

My begging technique was crudely simple. I merely presented myself at the back door and told the person who answered it, man, woman, or child, that I was hungry. A woman who sees a hungry teenaged boy at the door will, if she has anything to eat in the house at all, usually give him something. But as I mentioned earlier, many people in El Paso barely had enough for themselves. If a man was home during the daytime, and answered the door, the chances were very good that he was unemployed. In some instances, I am certain, an unemployed man gave me his lunch. But then, I was young, and it was easier for me to get fed than it was for an adult bum. And for Pearson, who was an adult, and also black, it was almost impossible to get a handout.

There are stages a man goes through. At first, when I had to descend to begging and panhandling, I was filled with shame. It took all of the courage I could muster to ding a stranger for a dime, a nickel, or anything. Then, after I had accepted the idea that I was a professional road kid—that begging was what I did—I didn't let anybody get by me. I asked everyone who came by for something: men, women, children, even the most unlikely prospects. If I was turned down when I asked for money, I asked for a cigarette. If I wasn't given a cigarette, I asked for a match, and failing to get a match, I would ask for directions or the time. It becomes a matter of perverse pride to get something from these strangers, your fellow Americans, even if it is only a curse. And even a curse isn't so bad because it is, at least, a recognition of sorts, a colorful and forceful acknowledgement of your existence.

But then, as time passes, a reaction sets in. Shame returns. Then when you have to beg for something, you wait until you truly have to beg, and you only approach the likeliest prospects, the people who will, more often than not, give you something to eat if they have it. How can you tell? I don't know, but after awhile, you can tell who they are by just looking at them.

Shame overwhelmed me in El Paso when I thought up what I considered to be a clever ruse. On the sidewalk, at the mouth of an alley, I placed a crust of bread I had saved from a sandwich. I hung back in the alley then, waiting until I saw a well-dressed man coming down the sidewalk. When he was level with the alley, I dived on the bread crust, and started gnawing at it as though I were ravenous. To my chagrin, the man laughed so hard he had to grab the lamp post to keep from falling.

114

"You're good, kid," he said, finally, wiping his streaming eyes, "you are really good!" Shaking his head, he walked away without looking back.

I was ashamed of myself, truly ashamed, and I never tried that ruse again—although I still think that it might have worked on an unsophisticated woman.

As I wandered the depressing streets of El Paso, certainly one of the most wretched cities in America, if not in the world, I constantly kept my eyes open for a cowboy hat for Billy Tyson. But as Billy had said, there didn't seem to be any way to get a cowboy hat without the money to buy one. Even in the Great Depression, a Stetson ten-gallon hat, at least the kind that Billy wanted, was twenty dollars. Hats were still sold in haberdasheries then, with only one front door, which made hats of any kind almost impossible to steal. At first, when I begged for food at a back door, I would ask the woman of the house if she had a spare cowboy hat. They invariably looked at me as if I were crazy, so I quit asking. I did, however, acquire a bright yellow rain slicker, a long, riding raincoat, the kind that spreads out in back, when unbuttoned, to cover the back of a saddle. This slicker kept the cold wind away from me at night, but during the day, as the sun grew warmer, it was too hot to wear because no air could get through the oilcloth.

At night the three of us would meet in Alligator Park. We would share our food with one another, if we had any, and then repair to the old tool shed behind the billboard, the haven I had discovered on my earlier visit to El Paso, and spend the night. Our three bodies, huddled together, warmed the small space. Rolled up in my crackling slicker, I could fall asleep easily on the wooden floor by nine P.M. and I would sleep soundly until the sun came up.

9

Billy Tyson, talking a blue streak (with most of his pitch, in all probability, incomprehensible) to the gentleman with the white Spitz, pestered the man until they reached the end of the gravel path and hit the sidewalk. Billy Tyson, shaking his head and pursing his lips, returned to our bench.

"He wouldn't give me nothen. A man who can afford to feed a dog oughta be able to give a man a lousy nickel and I told him so but he wouldn't give me shit."

Solemnly, Pearson held out his arm with his fist closed. "Who would like to go over to Juarez for some Mexican food?"

Pearson opened his fist and displayed a half-dollar on his palm. He had helped a man move a piano up two flights of stairs that morning, he told us, and the man had given him the half-dollar.

We had all been interested in going across the border to Juarez, but there was a two-cent toll for the bridge. It was also possible to ride the streetcar both ways across the bridge, but the two cents was added onto the cost of the token.

We walked, and made our way to the bridge through the El Paso streets, picking up a few strange looks from passersby along the way. Any one of us, walking alone, wouldn't have been given a second glance, but when the three of us were walking together, with our three different and novel ways of walking, we must have seemed peculiar. Billy Tyson, with his too-tight cowboy boots pinching his toes, tried to walk mostly on his heels because it was painful for him to jam his toes forward into the pointed ends of the boots if he put the soles down first. His boots still hurt

116

his feet, even when he walked on the high heels, but not as badly, he said. So Billy took short, almost mincing steps. Pearson, because he wore so many clothes, actually struggled as he walked. He stamped each foot down hard, with steps almost as short as Billy's, and he kept his fists clenched, holding his elbows well out from his thick, padded torso. I was still wearing the oversized golf shoes, so I had to shuffle along, barely lifting my heels from the sidewalk. The metal screwholes on the soles and heels of my shoes made loud scraping noises as well. My long gliding strides would usually put me well ahead of the other two in almost no time, and then I would have to stop and wait for them to catch up with me. So it is no wonder that some people, if not all of the passersby, looked at us strangely.

With some apprehension, after Pearson paid our fees, we crossed the bridge across the Rio Grande into Juarez. Compared with Agua Prieta, Juarez was a large, if hardly thriving, city. The streets were jam-packed with people, and Pearson and I were a little frightened by its foreignness. But the noise and the sinister-looking Mexicans didn't seem to bother Billy Tyson. He just chattered away, and pointed things out to us, as though we couldn't see anything for ourselves. We shopped along the main drag, looking for cheap prices. Then we went into a long narrow café that had a counter, and shared a plateful of tacos, with three bowls of beans apiece. After paying, Pearson still had a lot of change left.

A straight city can always stay straight as long as it has a sin city nearby. Columbus, Georgia, has Phenix City, Alabama; Pittsburgh has Steubenville, Ohio; and Los Angeles then had San Bernardino. (Today, of course, San Bernardino has Los Angeles.) Juarez served as El Paso's sin city, and if a visitor had money he could buy anything in Juarez then, from cocaine to sexual circuses. We admired

117

the posters outside a little theater that featured porno-graphic cartoons, but we didn't have enough money to go inside and see them. As we walked around after eating, eyeing the puny, ragged Mexicans and the skinny, begging children, we felt relatively well-off.

After walking up and down the main drag for about an hour (we didn't venture down any of the unlighted side streets), we began to get apprehensive about the possibility that we wouldn't be allowed to reenter the United States. We hadn't thought about it on the way over, but none of us had any identification to prove that we were U.S. citizens. Billy Tyson didn't worry or care. He figured that if we were turned back we could sneak across the river later that night, the way I had crossed back across the border in Agua Prieta. But there was no reentry problem. There was a constant stream of foot traffic on the bridge, with most of the pedestrians obviously Mexicans, and after Pearson paid the toll we were waved through both check-points without a word. After we were safely back, Pearson complained about the laxity of the border guards. If they made it hard for the Mexicans to get in, there wouldn't be so many Mexicans in El Paso, and it might be possible then for a colored man to get a job, he said. What he said was true enough, because there seemed to be a lot more Mex-icans than Americans in El Paso.

Later that night, after we got back to our tool shed, we had a long discussion about what we should do. Our wel-come was wearing out fast at the yard breadline, and we were in danger of being turned away. The man who ran it, a Christianized Texan who got various people and agen-cies around El Paso to contribute food, had made a couple of comments already about our daily appearance in the line. The breadline was supposed to be a stopgap relief handout for transients passing through El Paso, not a permanent feeding place for long-term residents. The idea was to give bums a meal at the yards so they would then catch the next train out of El Paso. So far, we hadn't been turned away, but the possibility was imminent.

Pearson knew a woman in East St. Louis, he said, who would probably put us up for a few days, but even if she was unwilling to take us in, we could live much more comfortably and eat a lot better than we could in El Paso. The city was larger, more prosperous, and there were not so many bums in competition for handouts in St. Louis as there were in El Paso. Then, when it got warmer, we could continue on our journey.

Billy had no valid objections to St. Louis, except to say that once he was out of the West, his chances of getting a cowboy hat would be much slimmer. But that wasn't so, Pearson explained. There were plenty of Stetsons in St. Louis, because that was the gateway to the West. Because the pickings were so much better there, we could pool and save our money as we panhandled it or earned it or stole it, and, after we amassed twenty dollars, we could *buy* Billy a cowboy hat, a new one, a hat that would fit his head exactly. I went along with this idea because, by now, I truly wanted Billy Tyson to have his cowboy hat so he could go home to Kentucky. Besides, once in St. Louis, I would be a lot closer to Chicago than I was here in El Paso, a city I detested.

The next day, we caught the noon freight for Alamagordo, New Mexico. We arrived at dusk, with about an hour's worth of gray light left in the red sky. On a small bluff, about two hundred yards away from the tracks, the U.S. government had set up a breadline, serving meat stew, bread, and individual pint bottles of milk. Some other bums, riding in our empty from El Paso, had told us about the breadline. In return for the free meal, each bum had to be interviewed first for some kind of federal survey before he could get the meal ticket. All of the Alamagordo residents knew about the breadline and the government project, so it was impossible to get a handout in town. The survey breadline, then, was the only place in town for a transient to get something to eat. That was why the government had chosen small towns like Alamagordo to make its surveys.

When the train stopped, for a scheduled half-hour makeover, there was a frenzied rush for the bluff. I became separated from Billy Tyson and Pearson because I couldn't run in my golf shoes without having them fall off. I could only shuffle along at an increased rate, and even so I lost one shoe climbing the bluff. By the time I retrieved the shoe, I ended up as the next to last man in the line. There were two interviewers, and the line moved right along. When I reached my interviewer, a man of about twenty-five or -six with hairy forearms and black-rimmed glasses, I sat across from him at the folding field table and accepted the tailor-made cigarette he offered me with sincere appreciation. It was the first tailor-made (a Camel) I had smoked in a long time, and it was voluptuously rich after smoking RJR flakes rolled in brown wheatstraw papers.

The interviewer was affable, proud of his job and the fact that he had one, I supposed. He asked my name and age. I said, "Jake Lowey," but when I told him I was seventeen he flinched slightly. Nevertheless, he wrote it down without calling me on it.

"What're your plans?" he asked, after licking the tip of his pencil.

"Well," I said, "what I'd like to do is to trade this yellow slicker I'm wearing for a Navy pea jacket. It's okay for now, the slicker, but when I get up to where the snow is, it'll probably crack on me."

"No, no," he said, shaking his head. "What I mean is, where are you going and what kind of work are you looking for?"

Perhaps I wanted to impress him—I'm not sure—but I did enjoy this personal interest he was taking in me; besides, he was so innocent and sincere I didn't want to let him down.

"Oh," I said, "radio. When I get to Chicago I'm going to go to radio school. I intend to be an announcer and a radio engineer. Radio seems like a good field, and I'm sure it would make a good career for me."

He became quite excited when I told him this, and he scribbled it all down on the government form. "I think that's wonderful," he said. "I've been interviewing—ah—transients for three weeks now, and you're the first young man who's told me he wanted to attend a trade school and improve his position. Almost everyone else says he wants to drive a truck or else work at anything he can find. So it's rather wonderful to encounter a—ah—young man who has faith in himself and in America. How's your math?"

"Who?"

"Math. Mathematics. In radio, you'll need a solid background in math."

"In school," I lied, "I always made straight A's in math."

He then opened a huge gray book, a catalogue with long listings of occupational specialties and schools, and told me about the educational possibilities in Chicago for school loans, and other opportunities in radio.

By the time he finished talking to me, and writing down some addresses of schools for me in Chicago, the chow was all gone, the train was made up, and I had to scramble down the bluff to catch the train. Billy Tyson, who had been eating outside the open food shed, and watching me with some concern during the long interview, had saved me a piece of bread.

"What happened?" he said, once the train was moving. "I thought you was in some kind of trouble."

"I don't know what happened. But when I told the guy I wanted to be a radio announcer, he got all excited and started in with all kinds of questions."

"God, you're dumb," Billy Tyson said. "You're supposed to say you wanta be a truck driver. That way, you can get it over with and eat."

I never saw the results of the survey, but I have wondered since how the bureaucrats in Washington ever explained the desire of six million men to drive trucks as a lifetime career.

The flurries of snow began before the train reached Tucumcari. The reddish, desolate New Mexico landscape, with distant pustules of crazily leaning redstone knobby pillars, together with the black sky and scattered bursts of snow that came suddenly from nowhere, reminded me of the landscapes Edgar Rice Burroughs described in his Mars novels. If Demos and Phobos had appeared, "hurtling," as Burroughs always described the two moons, "across the thin air," I wouldn't have been surprised. It became too cold to leave the sliding door to the freight car open, and someone rolled it shut. Then, because it was so dark inside the car, which made it seem even colder, we started stripping sheets of dark brown paper from the walls, tearing them into smaller bits, and we built little fires. We watched the tiny fires carefully, because of the wooden floor of the boxcar, but the sudden fast-burning spurts of fire were wonderful for the few moments that they lasted. Eventually, the interior of the empty was filled with smoke, and the supply of air was almost exhausted. Choking and coughing, we had to crack the door open again to let the smoke out and to obtain some fresh air.

Before the train stopped rolling in the Tucumcari yards, Pearson, Billy Tyson, and I dropped off the slowly moving car.

Pearson had been in Tucumcari before, and he wanted us to get to this bakery he knew about before any of the other bums got to it. Bakers work all night, and because there is always plenty of clean-up work to do, free help to do the dirty work is welcomed. In a small city like Tucumcari, with bums passing through every night, the fat baker who let us in through the back door never had to wash a single pan. While we were working in the big kitchen (about three hours), he turned four other volunteers away. Thanks to Pearson, we had got there first.

Before putting us to work, the baker fried eggs and bacon for us, and gave us a heaping plateful of hot cross buns fresh from the oven. The buns almost melted in my mouth, they were so fresh, light, and hot. I washed innumerable long flat baking pans, while Billy Tyson swept and mopped the floor. Pearson washed dishes, cleaned and polished the sinks, and moved supplies out of the storeroom for the baker. We stretched out our assigned tasks as long as possible, relishing the warmth and lovely odors of the huge kitchen. As I polished long flat pans with steel wool, I thought that this baker had the best job in the entire world. He was a kindly, paunchy man who evidently loved his work, and it was skilled work he could do all by himself in a warm comfortable room without any supervision. Now that I have lived long enough to indulge myself in the writing of an autobiography, I can say that the occupation of baker is one of the five best occupations in the world. The other four are infantry rifleman (Private); novelist; lighthouse keeper; and professional boxer. Of them all, rifleman is tops, of course, but I probably wouldn't admit that if I were not a professional novelist.

When we left, the baker gave each one of us a large sack of rolls, some hot cross buns, and coffee cakes. We had missed the train, and we spent the rest of the night huddling together in an empty boxcar on a siding. The warmth of the bakery had made the weather seem much colder outside, but it was still about the same in actual temperature. I found it difficult to judge the cold. In Tuc-umcari I was experiencing snow for the first time. I was overwhelmed by it, although it was scattered snow. The wind was so strong that the drifts were low and small. In the morning, when we had built a fire, and the southbound train from Dalhart came in, I had forebodings about the snow the new arrivals told us about up there in the Texas panhandle. Several shivering bums joined us at our fire, all of them anxious to get back on the southwest train that was bound for El Paso, and they thought we were crazy for wanting to travel northeast. But we three, with our recent and intimate knowledge of El Paso, thought they were equally crazy for traveling southwest. As cold as it was, although it was only about thirty degrees above zero, I could hardly stand the numbness of my fingers and toes; they felt as if they no longer belonged to me. My cracked lips had split even wider, and it was painful to compress my lips. I began to wonder how much more cold I could take if the temperature dropped to twenty, ten, zero, and then to below zero. But the weather, as everyone agreed, was unseasonable for March, and it was due to warm up any day now. Pearson's vivid depiction of the warmth and generosity of the prosperous people in St. Louis, a city we should reach within two or three days, overcame my better judgment, so when the next train left for Dalhart I climbed aboard.

Only three other men climbed into the empty with us, and they turned out to be hobos, not bums. They were going to Liberal, Kansas, to load winter wheat into boxcars, they said. When they described this work, the pushing of huge piles of wheat with shovels four feet wide, in choking wheat dust, to the back of each boxcar, with constantly shifting heaps of grain beneath their feet, I concluded that they were assholes for wanting jobs like that. And yet they seemed happy at the prospect of this back-breaking, mind-numbing employment. I couldn't understand how they, or anyone else, could do such work willingly, nor could I understand Pearson's desire to get a place on an automobile assembly line in Detroit. A man has little enough dignity in his life as it is, without becoming a part of a machine.

The worst weather was yet to come.

For the last five miles, going into Dalhart, the train struggled along at fewer than five miles an hour. We had encountered a blizzard, the kind that the Texas panhandlers call a Norther. The fat and heavy flakes of snow moved horizontally in gusts that must have reached, at times, about fifty miles an hour. As we took turns looking through the narrow slit in the slightly cracked door, all we could see was a massive wall of whiteness. Visibility was reduced to about ten yards, and I knew that if a man was out there in all that whiteness, out in a field somewhere, trying to run in that avalanche of snow, he would be buried under it and frozen as he ran before he could cover a hundred yards. When the train stopped in the Dalhart yards, we were afraid to get off. To keep from freezing, we kept running back and forth inside the car, the clouds of moisture steaming from our mouths and nostrils like engines. After about an hour, a brakeman, or a shack, as they are called, came along with a lantern and told us to stay where we were. There would be no more trains out of Dalhart in any direction, he said, until the tracks were cleared.

"If we stay here," one of the would-be wheat-shovelers whined, "we'll freeze to death."

"Just stay put," the shack repeated. "Somebody'll come for you all directly."

Another long cold hour passed. Then a man wearing a knee-length sheepskin coat did come for us. When he had collected all of the bums on the train—there were about thirty all told—he led us out of the yards and along the main drag to the courthouse. Ropes had been strung along the streets, tied to lampposts and fire hydrants, and stretched across intersections, so we could hang onto them without being blown away. We followed the man in single file, staying as close together as we could in the piledriving snowstorm. The drifts, on the southern side of the main drag, were almost as high as the second stories of the office buildings. My hands were completely numb, without gloves, and it was curious to watch my hand reach out and clutch a rope, grasp it, and see that I was holding onto it without being able to feel the rope.

I thought we were going to be put up in the jail, and I was looking forward to spending the night—or forever— in a warm jail cell, or anywhere, just to get out of the cold. But we were not taken to jail. We were lodged on the first floor, the icy cold marble floor, of the courthouse. The elevators were locked, and the stairway to the second floor was blocked off with a rope. The man who had led us there was a deputy sheriff, and he told us we could stay in the building, and sit or sleep on the floor, until the Norther had run its course.

A year earlier, he told us in a matter-of-fact voice, during the winter, there had been an equally strong Norther, and eighteen bums had been found frozen to death in boxcars after it was over. The city had had to bury these men, he said, and the city did not intend to go through that expense again. The courthouse was warm enough, and we were out of the wind, but the marble floor was too hard and cold to be comfortable. The pain in my cracked lower lip was almost unbearable. I dug around in my split lip with my thumbnail and picked out a round red stone. It was a frozen drop of blood, as red as a ruby. I placed it on the palm of my left hand, rubbed it with my thumb, and it melted into a streak of blood. The pain in my lower lip was greatly diminished, however, and feeling came back to my hands and feet.

A few minutes later, a Salvation Army captain arrived at the courthouse with a kettle of lukewarm chicken soup. He had carried the kettle for three blocks, and the heat was all but gone. There was no way to reheat it, and only a few men had any containers to drink it with, including Pearson, who had a cup in his bindle to dip into it. But cool chicken soup was better than nothing, and I took my turn with Pearson's scummy cup.

Pearson and Billy Tyson managed to fall asleep, but I could not. The snow was too strange, wonderful, and mysterious. I stood in the wide foyer, by the glass doors, looking out at the wall of white snow, watching it climb the broad steps until they were covered completely. I would turn away occasionally, afraid of my thoughts, and roll and smoke a matchstick-thin cigarette. Then I would be drawn back to the doorway again. What I wanted to do, or what I thought I wanted to do, was to be covered up by that cold white blanket. I recalled Jack London's short stories about the joy of freezing to death in Alaska: at first, the bitter, numbing cold, and then the sudden flush that got warmer and warmer until one fell, beautifully, into death itself, the most wonderful warmth of all. Finally, frightened by my dark thoughts, I engaged another sleepless bum in conversation, a man in his early twenties, who had long legs and arms, and a face with the texture and color of a pigskin football.

He had been in the army for the last three years, he told me, having joined because of a scandal. But now that enough time had passed for the scandal to blow over he was returning home to Lincoln, Nebraska.

"What was the scandal?" I asked.

He shrugged, and twisted his lips comically. "It was a silly thing, really, but at the time it seemed damned serious to me. I was at the movies, sitting up in the balcony. It was a matinee, and the house, including the balcony, was only about half-filled. A little Negro girl, about sixteen, propositioned me. I gave her a quarter, and she popped it into her mouth. Then we climbed up to the very last row, right under the projection booth. She bent over the seat row, and I dropped my pants and slipped it to her from behind. Well, at that exact time, the film broke, or the projector broke, I don't know which, and they turned the house lights on while they fixed it. Well, you know how people are. They all turned around in their seats to look up at the projection booth, as if they could see through the wall to find out what went wrong. But what they saw was me, with my pants down and my bare ass showing, pumping away on this little Negro girl. I pulled up my pants, ran down the stairs, and out of the theater. I hitch-hiked to Des Moines, and enlisted in the regular Army. It was the most awful thing that had ever happened to me. I was on the high school basketball team, you know, a

128 *A THEATER IN LINCOLN, NEBRASKA THAT WASN'T SEGREGATED!*

forward, and everybody in town knew me. A lot of my friends were in the audience, and so was my former history teacher, a very nice and respectable woman."

"If you wrote that story up," I said, "you could probably sell it for a lot of money to the *Reader's Digest*. They've got this regular section called, 'My Most Embarrassing Moment.'"

"No." He shook his head. "I'll never write it up. I still feel bad about it, even though the whole thing was kind of silly, you know. But after three years, I figure it'll all be blown over. Don't you think so?"

"Sure," I said. "Nobody'll remember that, not after three years." But I only said that to cheer him up. I don't think a scandal as juicy as that one would ever blow over in a little town like Lincoln, Nebraska.

We talked some more, and he told me that after a year in Fort Lewis, Washington, he had transferred down to Panama and put in two years with the 33rd Infantry Regiment. On a twenty-mile jungle hike, his company had encountered a tribe of San Blas Indians. The Indians had begged for soap, and then when the soldiers had given them some bars they had in their packs, the Indians ate the soap. They all wore big smiles as the slobbery soap bubbles dribbled down their chins.

"How could they eat soap? Soap tastes terrible."

"Not to a San Blas Indian, it don't. Their theory is that if it smells good, it tastes good, you see. And there's a certain logic to it, too, when you think about it. But San Blas Indians are different from us, you see, and they like to eat soap. That's what I learned in the Army."

"That's something interesting to know, I guess."

"It's plenty, but it was enough for me to know that I wanted to go home to Lincoln and stay there, anyway. If

I'd've reenlisted in the Army for another hitch, I'd've ended up as crazy as a San Blas Indian."

He stretched out then, all six-foot-two of him, and went to sleep. Toward dawn, after squeezing in between Pearson and Billy Tyson, I dozed off for awhile myself.

10

The next morning the snow had stopped falling and the wind had stopped blowing. The sky was still overcast and dark, and the light seemed to come from the snow instead of coming from above. Outside, the silence was immense, now that the wind had stopped. The only sounds were the squeaky–scrunchy noises under our feet as we made our way, as well as we could, to the Salvation Army office about three blocks away, where the captain had promised to give us coffee and donuts.

Not everyone went to the Salvation Army office. Four bums stayed behind, even though they wanted donuts and coffee as much as we did. But some bums, who have been on the road for a long time, have developed a hatred for the Salvation Army and for other religious missions that far outweighs their hunger. Many missions, and most Salvation Army posts, force men to pray, sing hymns, and listen to sermons before they will give them any food. This kind of coercion is, of course, the ultimate in humiliation and indignity to a man who is down on his luck. And some men, who have been far enough down to endure it once, will not go through this kind of humiliation again. But the prospect of singing and praying for something to eat has never bothered me. Basically, I think these God enthusiasts mean well, and the exchange of words for food is a fair one. In a way, when I exchange words for money, which I then use for food, I am doing the same thing in an indirect manner. Besides, I like to sing, and I especially like to sing hymns. Once, in a San Francisco mission, I sang "Power in the Blood" so loudly the preacher asked me to stop singing, and sent me to the kitchen to help out. And sermons are interesting, too, in an amusing way. One can enjoy a sermon for the speaker's technique if not for the content, the way one can enjoy a B movie for its technical aspects, even if the story is corny and uninteresting.

But there was no sermon and we were not asked to pray or sing. The captain, a poor man in a shabby uniform in an even poorer town, had a very small office, and no assembly hall. Recalling the soup from the night before, I had a hunch that he had to make a personal sacrifice to provide us with donuts and coffee. His office was hot and uncomfortable with so many men crowded together, but we lingered on long after the coffee and donuts were gone. There was nowhere else to go, unless we wanted to trudge back to the courthouse. Then the snowplows were working, and the streets were being cleared. A few businesses opened up, and the shopkeepers brought out their snow shovels.

"Let's go get us a shovel," Pearson said. Billy Tyson and I followed him outside.

We quickly found work shovelling the sidewalks. By noon, we had all made a little money from the shopkeepers. I had thirty cents, getting a dime from each store, and Billy had made the same amount. Pearson, of course, because of his blackness and challenging eyes, had collected fifty-five cents.

The cold afternoon air was still, and there was some difficulty in getting enough of it to breathe. It was as if the storm had taken most of the atmosphere along with it when it left the area, leaving only a minimal amount of thin air behind. Walking, stumbling mostly, and shovelling, had produced a thin film of sweat on my body beneath the yellow slicker. The temperature had climbed to twenty-five above zero.

We bought a dozen weenies and a damaged, discounted lemon cake at a small grocery store near the RR yards. We then went into the yards to eat and to check on yard activity and train schedules. A shack told us that there would definitely be a train out that evening going south, but he wasn't sure about any trains going to Kansas. He then told us to get the hell out of the yards and to stay as far away from the station as possible. Some bum had stolen the RR bull's lunch box and thermos from the station, and the bull was in an evil mood.

We returned to the courthouse, passing a few insane Dalhart residents in the streets who kept saying to one another: "Cold enough for you?"

"It can't git too cold for me!"

But all the same, the Dalhartians were good people. Three housewives, who had heard about the stranded bums in the courthouse, brought in a trayful of meatloaf sandwiches. Apparently, the memory of last winter's dead, frozen bums was still vivid in their minds. But this was something I didn't want to think about. If the deputy had not brought us to the courthouse the evening before, the three of us could have been found frozen to death, although I didn't really believe that it would have happened to me. Sooner or later, I think I would have left the boxcar and found shelter somewhere.

I was exhausted from lack of sleep, and from the unaccustomed work of shoveling. After eating a meatloaf sandwich, I went to sleep on the floor for the rest of the afternoon. When I awoke I was all alone in the courthouse. I was out of tobacco and papers. My muscles were stiff and sore from shovelling and the hard floor, and I was running a slight fever. Too tired to get up, I sat with my back against the wall, unable to focus my thoughts on anything, and not caring. The cold had numbed my mind and drained my will. My depression was bone-deep. The cold had deadened my heart.

Billy Tyson came for me. The southbound train for Tucumcari had already left, and most of the bums we had come into Dalhart with had taken it back to El Paso. But there were two more freights making up, the train to Topeka, Kansas, and the Ma Ferguson to Dallas. The Ma Ferguson had been named for the first woman governor of Texas, and it was reputed to be the fastest freight train in America. It went from Dalhart all the way down to Brownsville, Texas, on the Mexican border.

I told Billy Tyson that I would meet him and Pearson in the jungle past the water tower outside the yards, but I had to take a dump first, and then get a sack of Bull Durham or Golden Grain for the ride to Topeka. He took off, but I continued to sit there, too weary to move. I finally forced myself to stand, and once I got outside in the cold still air I began to feel myself again. The lights from a pool hall cast a golden light on the snowbank between the sidewalk and the street. I entered the pool room to use the john. There were about a dozen loungers in the pool hall, most of them elderly men sitting on high chairs, and all of them watching four younger men playing a game of snooker. The can was in the back, and no one paid any attention to me as I walked to the back of the long narrow room.

The cowboy hat was on a nail on the back of the unpainted door to the men's room. I didn't see it until I had entered and closed the door. It was the archetype of all jowboy hats: *the* cowboy hat. The color was a rich tobacco brown, although it was encrusted with dirt and dust. The brim, about four inches wide, was pinched in front to a nippled point. The sides were curled into rakish arabesques—just enough, but not too much. There was an inch-high rattlesnake skin hatband, and there were jagged peak and valley sweatmarks above the band. These glittering sweatmarks were salty white against the dark tobacco brown. There was a round hole in the crown. A bullet hole? There was also a leather thong that was loose in front, encircling the crown, with the two ends dropped down through two holes about midway back from the front of the crown. The ends of the thongs were long enough to be tied beneath the wearer's chin. I took the hat down from the nail and looked inside. It was a Stetson, size 7¼, and the perforated sweatband was maculate with hair oil. A few black curly hairs were caught in the sweatband. I tried it on, but the hat was too big for me. I unrolled some toilet paper and made four square pads, each one of them about an eighth of an inch thick. When I placed these pads under the sweatband, the hat fit my head beautifully. I tied the two loose ends of the thong under my chin.

Then I took a piss, and tried to think of what I had to do. I knew that I would take the hat, but I didn't know whether to wear it boldly and march out of the pool room, or hide it inside my shirt. It could belong to one of the pool players, or perhaps to the pool hall owner, a Greek-

134

looking man who sat behind a glass display counter of candy and tobacco at the front of the room by the door. With some reluctance, although I knew it wouldn't injure the hat, I crushed it as flat as I could, unbuttoned my shirt, and shoved it around to the back. I buttoned my yellow slicker, which was loose-fitting anyway, and I didn't think the slight bulge on my back would be noticeable. I unlocked the door, and forced myself to saunter through the pool room to the front counter. I put a nickel on the glass top, and asked for a sack of Golden Grain and some extra cigarette papers.

The proprietor, a heavy set, middle-aged man, with a tonsure of thick black hair surrounding a dead white dome, shoved the sack of tobacco toward me and gave me an extra sheaf of papers. He didn't touch my nickel, but looked into my eyes. He had the wet black eyes of a wolf.

"You gotta place to stay tonight, kid? I close at eleven."

"I'll be back," I lied, and I pocketed my nickel.

I turned right, instead of going toward the yards, and circled the block before heading for the tracks. I hoped that by turning right I had thrown him off. When the owner of that hat inquired, if he did, the proprietor would point him in the wrong direction.

I truly wanted to keep that cowboy hat. I had stolen it, and it was mine—not Billy Tyson's. So why shouldn't I keep it? I could begin a new quest of my own for cowboy denims and boots, and then return to Los Angeles and tell all my friends that I had been a cowboy out West myself. Whether one lived back East in Kentucky, or out in California, as far west as anyone could ever get, the real West was always that indefinite area of Texas-Arizona-New-and-Old Mexico, although there was no true West. It was the imaginary West of myth and movies, and I suppose it always had been. O God but I wanted to keep that hat! But

I could not. To do so would be stealing another man's dream. And the dream was Billy Tyson's, not mine.

Pearson and Billy Tyson were about fifty yards away from the water tower, and well back from the tracks. Pearson had boiled some coffee in his tin can, and they had saved me a hunk of the lemon cake. I hunkered down by the fire and ate the cake, still reluctant to part with the cowboy hat.

All of the tracks were clear now, Pearson said, and there would be extra sections for all trains, both passenger and freights, to make up for the lost shipments.

"Including another train back to El Paso?"

"Uh huh. The shack said 'after midnight.' "

I unbuttoned my slicker, and then my shirt. I reached around inside and pulled out the beautiful hat. After I pushed out the crown to make the hat resume its shape, I shoved it out ungraciously to Billy Tyson.

"Here," I said. "Here's your fucken cowboy hat."

Billy started to cry. He gently pooched in a couple of dents in the crown, and put on the hat. It had been too big for me, and it was too big for Billy, but a little more paper inside the sweatband would take care of the fit.

"Now I can go home," Billy said, wiping his eyes with his dirty fingers.

When he said that, I knew that I could also go home if I wanted to, although I didn't know what I wanted to do at the moment. What I did know was that I was a loser. A winner would have kept the cowboy hat for himself. But I hadn't wanted it badly enough. I had never wanted anything badly enough to make an all-out effort to obtain it, and I knew that I would always be that way, for the rest of my life. And I didn't care, because, in a way, it was a relief, a comfort to know something so important about myself. And I was very happy that Billy Tyson could now go home.

Pearson and I saw Billy off on the Ma Ferguson. He was the only rider on a flat car that also carried several piles of lumber.

"Watch out for Texas Slim going through Longview, Billy," I said.

Billy pushed his hat back and grinned. "He better watch out for me!"

Pearson and I went back to the fire.

"That was a good thing you done," Pearson said, "given Billy the hat. You wanted it yourself, didn't you?"

I nodded. "But not as bad as Billy."

"Me, too." Pearson laughed, the first time I had heard him laugh since I had stumbled naked into the Douglas jungle. "I'd've traded my Borsalino for it."

But I didn't believe him. I don't think Pearson would have traded his Borsalino for anything. He knew too much about hats for that. He knew as much about hats as I did.

Pearson then tried, although his heart wasn't in it, to talk me into going to St. Louis with him. But I wouldn't go. Pearson left on the freight for Topeka, and eventually, I hope, for Detroit and his job on the assembly line.

I had told Pearson and Billy Tyson that I was going South where it was warm, and that when I got warm again I was going to stay warm. I no longer cared if I ever got to Chicago and the World's Fair.

At midnight I was alone by the fire and missing my friends already, but I was much happier alone, and I knew it.

Now that I no longer had the responsibility for Billy Tyson or Pearson I could go to Mobile or New Orleans and ship out on a freighter for South America. If I could learn how to drive a car I could go to Miami Beach, maybe, and drive a taxicab. Or I could go to San Francisco, or Seattle, or Alaska. Alaska? Why not Alaska, that is, if I could get a good used Navy pea jacket first. My possibilities were limitless. One man alone, without responsibilities, has got a fighting chance in this world; and it was, indeed, a wonderful world.

PART THREE

CODA

CAPRICORNUS

Today at sixty, alive,
I am father to the father,
Dead at thirty—one-half century defunct—
Defunct with all of its connotations.
Fairly or unfairly, I've blamed you
For my birth,
For my deliberate abandonment
At the age of two.
But now I must confront you squarely.
Is it fair to blame you,
A headstrong, emotional young man,
A young man desiring immortality,
For my birth, my hunger, my war wounds,
For my absent superego,
For my deliberate decision
To deny you your desired immortality
By refusing to father a son?

You, dead father, are now my son—
How do you like it now, old man?
Young man? Poor misguided progenitor.
By denying you, did I deny myself?
No, I think not, I know not,
Because I still have you,
My father, my son.

I am looking at your picture:
In this faded photo your eyes are brown,

Although I know they're as blue as mine.
You are smiling. Thanks for that:
I still have your tombstone teeth.
You hold a straw boater in your hand,
and your handsome balding head shines.
My own glabrous skull
(if you could see it)
Could have been your own
If you had lived. But you did not.
When I was born, old man, you were twenty-eight.
At twenty-eight, you were dying with T.B.
You knew you wouldn't live to be bald,
To be responsible for me, your son.
You had me deliberately, recklessly,
Irresponsibly—and you never told my mother
That you had T.B.—that you were dying.
And so, poor woman, she died too,
Dead from the same dread disease.
This left me, then, an orphan,
At the age of eight,
Fatherless, motherless, and
Without a superego, without a prayer,
Without a religion, without a memory—
Except for this fading browntone photo.

What were you thinking about
When you had this studio portrait taken?
About your good looks?
(You kept them for yourself—
I could have used those good looks.)
There you stand, straight and tall,
The famous candy salesman.
You sold Whitman's chocolates
In Arizona, California, and Nevada

To support your stays in sanatoriums.
Do you know (of course you can't know)
How much I hated telling people
That my father was a candy salesman?
And yet, my snobbishness came from you, too,
Simply because you attended Chapel Hill.

With your dark jacket and white vest,
You support a watch and chain.
What happened to the gold watch?
At sixty, I should be entitled to the watch,
But from you I inherited nothing
Tangible, although my grandmother said
That my glibness came from you,
That, and my fierce blue eyes.
Well, that is something, not nothing.
I cannot hate the young man in the photo.
I must make peace with you
To make peace with myself.

Alone in the world,
I became stronger than you.
To overcome bitterness,
I developed a sense of humor.
To cheat you of your immortality,
I wrote books instead of siring children
(Although they were not published
On acid-free paper).

My search for a father has ended,
And I have beaten you, old man, young man.
I am the small winner here,
And you, Papa, are the loser.

—Or am I?

Charles Willeford (1919-1988) served in the U.S. Army and the Air Corps for twenty years, retiring as a master sergeant. As a tank commander with the 10th Armored Division in the Second World War, he was awarded the Silver Star, the Bronze Star for valor, the Purple Heart with one oak leaf cluster, and (during the Battle of the Bulge) the Luxembourg Croix de Guerre. He subsequently served as a rifle company sergeant with the Army of Occupation in Japan, and as an Air Force base historian.

After leaving the service, he became a professor of English at the University of Miami and Miami-Dade Community College. Mr. Willeford was the author of twenty novels, and several works of criticism and non-fiction. In addition, he wrote the screenplay for the film of his novel *Cockfighter*, in which he also acted. His wife, Betsy, is an editorial writer for *The Miami News*.